POLITICAL AGENDAS FOR EDUCATION

"Now, more than ever, the understanding of politics in education is critical if public education is to survive. Spring's analyses provide background and insight that is essential for all teachers and administrators to understand. This is an essential text for all educators to read and learn."

—Rosemary Papa, Northern Arizona University, USA

Following the epic, contentious 2016 presidential election, Joel Spring's ongoing documentation and analysis of political agendas for education reflect the major political issues since 2012. Here he examines the 2016 education planks of the Republican, Democratic, Libertarian, and Green Parties, using their official platforms and other statements, speeches given by each candidate, and media reports and publications. Each party's position is linked to previous political movements in education. Spring offers an alternative agenda for American schools, including a proposed education amendment to the U.S. Constitution and replacing human capital agendas with goals emphasizing education for a long life and happiness. Taking a fresh look at the social and political forces, educational research, and ideologies shaping their educational agendas and a comparative approach, the book stimulates reflection and discussion.

Updates and changes in the Sixth Edition:

- Betsy DeVos's education agenda supporting vouchers, free market competition and for-profit schools and its relationship to the education section of the 2016 Republican platform
- The important role religion and culture played in the evolution of Republican education policies after the school prayer and Bible decisions of the 1960s
- The influence of human capital economics on Democratic education proposals
- How No Child Left Behind and Democratic President Barack Obama opened doors to the growth of the for-profit education industry and investment bankers
- The 2016 Democratic positions on the cost of higher education and student loan debts
- The Democratic left as represented by the 2016 campaign of Democrat Bernie Sanders and his influence on the presidential candidate Hillary Clinton and the Democratic Party platform
- The education proposals of the Green and Libertarian parties

Joel Spring is Professor at Queens College and the Graduate Center of the City University of New York, USA.

Sociocultural, Political, and Historical Studies in Education

Joel Spring, Editor

For a full list of titles in this series, please visit www.routledge.com/series/ LEASPHSES

Spring • *Political Agendas for Education: From Make America Great Again to Stronger Together, Sixth Edition*

Reagan • *Non-Western Educational Traditions: Local Approaches to Educational Thought and Practice, Fourth Edition*

Spring/Frankson/McCallum/Banks, Eds. • *The Business of Education: Networks of Power and Wealth in America*

Bowers • *A Critical Examination of STEM: Issues and Challenges*

Spring • *Deculturalization and the Struggle for Equality: A Brief History of the Education of Dominated Cultures in the United States, Eighth Edition*

Spring • *American Education, Seventeenth Edition*

Spring • *Economization of Education: Schools, Corporations, World Markets*

Martusewicz/Edmundson/Lupinacci • *EcoJustice Education: Toward Diverse, Democratic, and Sustainable Communities, Second Edition*

Spring • *Globalization and Education, Second Edition*

For additional information on titles in the Sociocultural, Political, and Historical Studies in Education series visit **www.routledge.com/education**

POLITICAL AGENDAS FOR EDUCATION

From Make America Great Again to Stronger Together

Sixth Edition

Joel Spring

 Routledge
Taylor & Francis Group

NEW YORK AND LONDON

First published 2018
by Routledge
711 Third Avenue, New York, NY 10017

and by Routledge
2 Park Square, Milton Park, Abingdon, Oxon, OX14 4RN

Routledge is an imprint of the Taylor & Francis Group, an informa business

© 2018 Taylor & Francis

Library of Congress Cataloging-in-Publication Data
A catalog record for this book has been requested

ISBN: 978-1-138-04107-3 (hbk)
ISBN: 978-1-138-04110-3 (pbk)
ISBN: 978-1-315-17467-9 (ebk)

Typeset in Bembo
by Apex CoVantage, LLC

BRIEF CONTENTS

CONTENTS

PREFACE

In the U.S. Senate on February 7, 2017, Vice President Mike Pence was forced to cast a historic tie-breaking vote to ensure the nomination of Betsy DeVos as U.S. Secretary of Education. During a tumultuous Senate hearing on DeVos's candidacy, Democratic members of the Senate Committee on Health, Education, Labor & Pensions and two Republicans refused to back her nomination because they considered her unqualified for the position.[1] Betsy DeVos's appointment and the 2016 Democratic platform and Democratic nominee Hillary Clinton's campaign, as I discuss in this book, represent major breaks with the testing and standards movement embodied in the federal legislation No Child Left Behind and Democratic President Barack Obama's Race to the Top.

Chapter 1 focuses on Betsy DeVos's education agenda supporting vouchers, free market competition and for-profit schools and its relationship to the education section of the 2016 Republican platform. I elaborate on the influence of free market theory since the 1950s when Milton Friedman first proposed school competition using vouchers. Important in both the 2016 Republican platform and U.S. Secretary of Education Betsy DeVos's agenda is the championing of Christian values in schools. Foundations and think tanks, such as the Heritage Foundation, as I discuss in this chapter, played an important role in spreading ideas of vouchers and competition in education.

Chapter 2 discusses the important role religion and culture played in the evolution of Republican education policies after the school prayer and Bible decisions of the 1960s. One result was the inclusion of a school prayer section to the federal legislation No Child Left Behind. Republicans in the 20th and 21st centuries were also concerned with bilingual and multicultural education, contributing to calls for standardizing the curriculum and emphasizing English only rather than maintaining a variety of languages and cultures in schools.

Chapter 3 discusses the influence of human capital economics on Democratic education proposals. This is reflected in the 2016 Democratic platform's proposals for preschool education and higher education. Breaking with both No Child Left Behind and President Barack Obama's Race to the Top, Democratic presidential nominee Hillary Clinton and the Democratic platform gave no support to standardized testing and curricula in schools.

Chapter 4 shows how No Child Left Behind and Democratic President Barack Obama opened door to the growth of the for-profit education industry and investment bankers. It also deals with the 2016 Democratic positions on the cost of higher education and student loan debts.

In Chapter 5, I discuss the Democratic left as represented by the 2016 campaign of Democrat Bernie Sanders and his influence on the presidential candidate Hillary Clinton and the Democratic Party platform. Also, I review the education proposals of the Green and Libertarian parties.

In Chapter 6, I offer an alternative agenda for American schools, including a proposed education amendment to the U.S. Constitution and replacing human capital goals with one emphasizing education for long life and happiness.

Note

1 U.S. Congress, Senate Committee on Health, Education, Labor & Pensions, "Full Committee Hearing Nomination of Betsy DeVos." Retrieved from www.help.senate.gov/hearings/nomination-of-betsy-devos-to-serve-as-secretary-of-education on February 7, 2017.

1

THE REPUBLICAN EDUCATION AGENDA

Free Markets and Religion

Advocates of free markets and liberty, the basis of Republican support of school choice, are faced with the problem of ensuring that free markets do not result in chaos and violence. Some people could pursue their self-interest in the marketplace motivated by greed and unhindered by morality. The answer, as reflected in the 2016 Republican platform, is that religion and the family will instill values that will ensure ethical behavior in the pursuit of self-interest: "As George Washington taught, 'religion and morality are indispensable supports' to a free society."[1] In protesting same-sex marriages, the Republican platform stresses the importance of the family in maintaining national morality: "Traditional marriage and family, based on marriage between one man and one woman, is the *foundation for a free society* and has for millennia been entrusted with rearing children and *instilling cultural values* [author's emphasis]."[2]

This is what Trump adviser Steven Bannon calls "humane capitalism" supported by Christian values. Writing in the *New York Times*, David Brooks explains Bannon's views,

> Once there was a collection of Judeo-Christian nation-states, Bannon argue[s], that practiced a humane form of biblical capitalism and fostered culturally coherent communities. But in the past few decades, the party of Davos [a reference to the World Economic Forum]—with its globalism, relativism, pluralism and diversity—has sapped away the moral foundations of this Judeo-Christian way of life. Humane capitalism has been replaced by the savage capitalism that brought us the financial crisis. National democracy has been replaced by a crony-capitalist network of global elites. Traditional virtue has been replaced by abortion and gay marriage. Sovereign nation-states are being replaced by hapless multilateral organizations like the E.U.[3]

Describing Donald Trump's selection of Betsy DeVos as Secretary of Education, New York University historian Kim Phillips-Fein stated, "They [Betsy DeVos and husband Richard DeVos) have this moralized sense of the free market that leads to this total program to turn back the ideas of the New Deal, the welfare state."[4] As reported in the *New York Times Magazine*, Betsy DeVos believes a free market ideology can "advance God's kingdom."[5]

To ensure the ethical functioning of school choice and free markets requires, from this perspective, the instilling of religious and family values. These ideas came together in the 2016 election of President Donald Trump and the selection of Betsy DeVos as Secretary of Education. The 2016 Republican national platform highlighted free markets in education: "We support options for learning, including home-schooling, career and technical education, private or parochial schools, magnet schools, charter schools, online learning, and early-college high schools. We especially support the innovative financing mechanisms that make options available to all children: education savings accounts (ESAs), vouchers, and tuition tax credits."[6] And, in its continuing concern about the place of Christianity in education, the platform stated: "A good understanding of the Bible being indispensable for the development of an educated citizenry, we encourage state legislatures to offer the Bible in a literature curriculum as an elective in America's high schools."[7]

Education savings accounts (ESAs), vouchers and tuition tax credits are the three major family choice methods advocated by the Republican Party. Simply stated, "vouchers" given by state governments to families would allow them to choose between public, private and charter schools. The school given the voucher would receive state support. Tuition tax credits would give parents a tax credit for money spent on their child's schooling. Education savings accounts (ESAs) involve states depositing money they would have spent on a student's public school education into parent-controlled savings accounts to be used for tuition at a private school, online learning or for buying other educational materials.

The concern about religion and free enterprise in education were central to schooling concerns of President Trump's selection of U.S. Secretary of Education Betsy DeVos. Born Betsy Prince, she attended Michigan Christian schools: the Holland Christian School and Calvin College. The Holland Christian Schools' mission is to educate students to be:

> **Biblically Discerning-**Possess a knowledge of God's Word; understand and able to defend a Biblical worldview; able to critically evaluate the current culture in light of God's Word. **Spiritually Growing-**Have a vibrant, growing relationship with God the Father, Son, and Holy Spirit. Understand their God-given design and desire to serve Jesus Christ in whatever they do.[8]

Calvin College proclaims: "Calvin's identity is a Christian academic community dedicated to rigorous intellectual inquiry."[9]

With her husband, Richard DeVos, in 1992, they established the Dick and Betsy DeVos Family Foundation, which, in 2010, funded the American Foundation for Children. Similar to the 2016 Republican platform, the major goal of the American Foundation for Children was supporting state legislators who advocate school choice plans using vouchers, tuition tax credits, education savings accounts and the expansion of charter schools, especially for-profit charter schools.

The couple's combined inheritances were revenue sources for the Dick and Betsy DeVos Family Foundation. Richard DeVos, inherited part of the Amway fortune of $5.1 billion from his father Richard DeVos, Sr. Betsy (Prince) DeVos received an inheritance from her father's estate of $1.35 billion. "The couple," according to one report, "gave $5.2 million to the foundation in 2002, $10 million in 2003 and $14 million in 2004."[10] Dick DeVos said, "We have not hidden the fact by laying out in our disclosure that we have been blessed financially. Part of that responsibility is to be a blessing to others."[11]

"Following in the footsteps of our parents," the couple posted on the foundation's website, "we aim to be faithful servants. Our work focuses on education, community, the arts, justice, and leadership."[12]

Both dedicated Christians, they want to stop same-sex marriage—in 2004 they sponsored an amendment to the Michigan Constitution banning same-sex marriage—and to implement school choice.[13] The advocacy of school choice reflected Richard DeVos's dedication to free market economics. In addition, school choice would, they hope, allow parents to choose Christian-oriented schools.

Richard DeVos's support of school choice and for-profit schools is reflected in his attendance at Michigan's Northwood University where he funded a school of management named after him. The stated mission of the university is: "To develop the future leaders of a global, free-enterprise society. We believe in: The advantages of an entrepreneurial, free-enterprise society. . . . The Northwood idea: Bringing the lessons of the America free-enterprise society into the college classroom."[14]

The idea of for-profit schools competing in a marketplace supported by government funds, particularly as vouchers or as charter schools, was highlighted by President Donald Trump's speech on September 8, 2016, at the for-profit charter school Cleveland Arts and Social Science Academy. In the speech, President Trump praised the owner Ron Packard as representing the entrepreneurial spirit behind for-profit charter schools. In turn, Packard praised candidate Trump. Packard owns the Cleveland Arts and Social Science Academy through his company AACEL. The company operates 25 schools across the nation serving 8,500 students.[15] Ron Packard also owns K12 Virtual Schools, which manages online schools and sells online courses through its website.[16] K12's revenue in 2013 was $20.3 million. Working with Safanad Limited, a global investment firm with offices in Dubai and New York, Packard created Pansophic Learning, which absorbed K12. Kamal Bahamdan, CEO of Safanad, said, "Pansophic Learning exemplifies Safanad's commitment to visionary and high-value investments in education that help improve the lives of children and students globally. We feel fortunate to be able to back Ron and his team who have proven entrepreneurial and leadership skills in the sector to embark on such an important mission."[17]

U.S. Secretary of Education Betsy DeVos received support from Vice President Mike Pence, who as Governor of Indiana in 2012 greatly expanded the voucher system created by his predecessor Governor Mitch Daniels. Under Daniels, a student receiving a voucher for 90 percent of a private school tuition had to be from a low-income family as determined by eligibility for free or reduced lunch. When Governor Pence took office, he worked to expand vouchers to cover 50 percent of private school tuition for families earning $67,000 to $90,000, with no limits on the number of private school vouchers they could issue.[18] Similar to Betsy DeVos, Pence opposes same-sex marriages. As reported by *Time* magazine, Pence, in a speech opposing same-sex marriage, warned: "societal collapse was always brought about following an advent of the deterioration of marriage and family."[19]

In this chapter, I will focus on arguments for a free market in education with for-profit schools funded by vouchers, tuition tax credits and education savings accounts. In Chapter 2, I will discuss religion and education and the Republican education agenda.

School Choice, Free Market Theory and the Republican Education Agenda

Economist Milton Friedman, influenced by Austrian economist Friedrich Hayek, was the first proponent of a U.S. school voucher.[20] In their most radical anarcho-libertarian form, Austrian economists such as Murray Rothbard advocated abolishing all forms of government and applying free market theory to every aspect of living, including highways, law enforcement, defense and schooling through privatization of government services, including schools.[21] Without government interference, these Austrian economists argued, marketplace competition would create ideal institutions. Applied to schooling, this meant no government provision or control of education. Instead, entrepreneurs would organize schools and compete for students. Competition or the "invisible hand" of the marketplace was to determine the best schools.

Hayek's economic ideas played a major role in the Reagan-style Republican-ism of the 1980s and 1990s and in conservative attacks on liberalism and government bureaucracy. In the 1930s, Hayek debated English economist John Maynard Keynes over the role of government in a capitalist system. Keynes argued that, for capitalism to survive, governments needed to intervene in the economy. Classical liberals, such as John Stuart Mill, opposed government intervention, but the progressive liberals of the 1930s justified government intervention to ensure equality of opportunity and provide a social safety net as necessary for the survival of capitalism.[22]

In *The Road to Serfdom*, Hayek set the stage for later conservative criticisms of government bureaucracies, including educational bureaucracies. He argued that the difficulty of determining prices or the value of goods would inevitably cause the failure of centrally planned economies. According to Hayek, pricing determines the social value of goods: What should a car cost in relation to food? What should the price of health care be in relation to education? In a free market, Hayek asserted, prices or social values are determined by individual choice. In a planned economy, pricing or social value is determined by a government bureaucracy. What criterion is used by a government bureaucracy? Hayek's answer was that the inevitable criterion is one that promotes the personal advantage of bureaucracy members. Bureaucrats and intellectuals supported by a bureaucracy, he argued, will advance social theories that vindicate the continued existence and expansion of the bureaucracy.[23]

Defining the enemy as the bureaucracy is one of Hayek's enduring legacies. Many educational critics complain that the problem with public schools is the educational bureaucracy. A frequently heard statement regarding schools is: "The problem is not money! The problem is bureaucratic waste!" By placing the blame on the educational bureaucracy, school reformers can avoid the issue of equal funding among school districts. Some public school students receive the benefits of living in well-financed suburban school districts, whereas others languish in overcrowded classrooms in poorly funded school districts that lack adequate textbooks and educational materials. Blaming the bureaucracy became an easy method for avoiding increased educational funding.

Beginning in the 1950s and lasting into the 21st century, many Republicans criticized the control of schools by a self-serving educational bureaucracy. In addition, as discussed in Chapter 2, some Republicans insisted that a liberal elite controlled the culture of universities, public schools and the media. Hayek identified these liberal elite as a new class composed of government experts and their intellectual supporters. Within this framework, schools could improve only if the power of the educational bureaucrats was broken and schools functioned according to the dictates of market competition.

Milton Friedman, a colleague of Hayek's at the University of Chicago and 1976 Nobel Prize winner, first advocated school vouchers to improve the education of low-income students. In contrast to those committed to a complete free market for schools, Friedman argued that the benefits of maintaining a stable and democratic society justified government support of education, but not government-operated schools. Friedman proposed a government-financed voucher that parents could redeem "for a specified maximum sum per child per years if spent on 'approved' educational services."[24] Friedman believed the resulting competition between private schools for government vouchers would improve the quality of education.

Also, Friedman contended in the 1960s that vouchers would overcome the class stratification that results from the existence of rich and poor school districts. Friedman suggested, "Under present arrangements, stratification of residential areas effectively restricts the intermingling of children from decidedly different backgrounds."[25] Except for a few parochial schools, Friedman argued, private schools were too expensive for most families, which resulted in further social class divisions in education.

Like Friedman, many Republicans embraced the free market but rejected the idea of completely abandoning government control, particularly social and moral control. After the riots and student rebellions of the 1960s and 1970s, Republicans believed that the government should exercise moral authority over social life. Free market ideologists contended that competition in the education market will result in improving the quality of education available to the American public. An unusual aspect of this argument is the support given to for-profit education. It is argued that a for-profit school will be more attuned to balancing costs with quality school instruction while trying to please parents. A for-profit education institution would want to market a good product to attract customers and control costs to ensure a profit.

Republicans worked to include for-profit education in the 2001 federal legislation called No Child Left Behind (NCLB) (signed into law on January 8, 2002). The stated purpose of NCLB was: "Improving the Academic Achievement of the Disadvantaged."[26]

Scattered throughout No Child Left Behind are provisions to support for-profit companies. For instance, the legislation states that assistance to schools requiring improvement because of low test scores can be provided by a "for-profit agency."[27] Under the Reading First section, reading and literacy partnerships can be established between school districts and for-profit companies.[28] Also, state and local school districts are provided funds to contract with for-profit companies to provide advanced placement courses and services; to reform teacher and principal certification; to recruit "highly qualified teachers, including specialists in core academic subjects, principals, and pupil services personnel"; "to improve science and mathematics curriculum and instruction"; "to develop State and local teacher corps or other programs to establish, expand, and enhance teacher recruitment and retention efforts"; to integrate "proven teaching practices into instruction"; for professional development programs; to provide services to teachers of limited English proficient students and for developing and implementing programs for limited English proficient students; to create and expand community technology centers; to accredit basic education of Indian children in Bureau of Indian Affairs Schools; and to train prospective teachers in advanced technology.[29]

For-profit schools were closely tied to the development of charter schools. Educational entrepreneur Chris Whittle proposed franchising for-profit schools. In the late 1980s, Whittle supported a federal government school vouchers. Whittle wanted to capture some of this voucher money by designing a conservative and technologically advanced school that could be franchised across the country.[30]

Politically, Whittle is a Republican. He made his position in the culture wars evident when he convinced the Federal Express Corporation to help fund the publication of Schlesinger's attack on multicultural education *The Disuniting of*

America.[31] Schlesinger's book carries the imprint of Whittle Direct Books and has full-page ads for Federal Express scattered through the text. Whittle tried to ensure that Schlesinger's educational ideas received a wide audience by sending free copies to business leaders around the country.

Whittle's political views are exemplified by his selection of the conservative president of Yale University, Benno Schmidt, to head his for-profit school enterprise. Whittle made the decision to hire Schmidt over food and drinks at a party in the ultra-exclusive Hamptons on Long Island. Offered an annual salary of about $1 million, Schmidt left Yale in 1992 to head what was called the Edison Project.[32]

Part of Whittle's plans went awry with the 1992 election of President Clinton, which ended an early effort by President George W. H. Bush to provide government-financed public-private school vouchers.[33] Without public-private school vouchers, the only hope for the Edison Project was to franchise private schools that were dependent on tuition income or to seek some other form of public support. The opportunity for public support came, according to the *New York Times Magazine* reporter James Traub, when "governors William Weld of Massachusetts and Buddy Roemer of Colorado contacted Schmidt in the fall of 1992 that they would like to find a way to bring Edison into the public schools in their states. Both states went on to pass 'charter school' laws that permit states and school systems to award contracts to . . . private contractors."[34] With charter schools, the operation of for-profit schools became a possibility.

Edison schools are an example of a leading for-profit education company. In 2008, the company was renamed EdisonLearning after it acquired a for-profit education software company. This acquisition is described in a corporate announcement.

> In 2008, a major company transformation took place with the . . . acquisition of the education software company Provost Systems, EdisonLearning combines its experience and core competencies in teaching and learning with a fully integrated online and Web-based technology solution that can dramatically achieve universal student access to a genuine, individualized learning experience.[35]

In 2013, EdisonLearning acknowledged its pioneering role in developing charter schools and its global reach.

> EdisonLearning is a leading international educational solutions provider with nearly 20 years of experience partnering with schools, districts, governments, organizations, charter authorizers, and boards. We *pioneered the concept of charter schools in the U.S.* . . . Since our founding, EdisonLearning has educated more than one million students, and currently serves partners with more than 450,000 students in 25 states, the United Kingdom and the Middle East through 391 school partnerships.[36]

In 2016, EdisonLearning defined its mission as: "We strive to shape a world in which every student, regardless of socioeconomic circumstance, has access to an excellent education and the ability to attain life skills that unlock their potential to powerfully impact our global society."[37] According to EdisonLearning: "During the 2015–16 school year, EdisonLearning is partnering with more than 350 schools in the United States, the United Kingdom, and Africa. Through these partnerships, EdisonLearning is helping to educate more than 150,000 students."[38]

Republicans advocating school choice had to convince the public, politicians and educators that public schools were resulting in low-quality education. Free markets and competition, they claimed would lift educational quality to new heights. As described in the next sections, selling the idea of educational free markets was done by a combination of conservative think tanks, foundations and Christian organizations.

Planning a Choice Revolution: The Trickle-Down Theory of Ideas, Foundations and Think Tanks

Conscience efforts were made to convince the public of the value of vouchers and free markets by conservative private foundations. My first realization of this attempt to revolutionize education occurred in the early 1970s at a meeting at the Institute for Humane Studies in Menlo Park, California. Discussion at the meeting focused on how to organize a cadre of intellectuals to openly support freedom and capitalism because, they believed, colleges and universities were hopelessly controlled by left-wing intellectuals. I was one of those academics, they hoped, who could be persuaded to spread free market ideas into academic establishments and to policymakers. Being elitists, these conservatives wanted to focus their efforts on intellectual and political leaders. Just as supply-side economists would later talk about trickle-down economics, these conservatives believed in trickle-down ideas.

At the time, I did not understand this as a movement later described by James Smith in *The Idea Brokers* (1991): "In the early 1970s, executives in a handful of traditionally conservative foundations redefined their programs with the aim of shaping the public policy agenda and constructing a network of conservative institutions and scholars."[39] William Simon was a leader and spokesperson for the movement. He left his job in 1976 as Secretary of the Treasury in the Nixon and Ford administrations to become head of the John Olin Foundation, the purpose of which, in Simon's words, "is to support those individuals and institutions who are working to strengthen the free enterprise system."[40]

Reflecting Simon's economic beliefs, the preface and foreword for his book *A Time for Truth* were written, respectively, by Milton Friedman and Friedrich Hayek. In the preface, Friedman sounded the warning that intellectual life in the United States was under the control of "socialists and interventionists, who have wrongfully appropriated in this country the noble label 'liberal' and who have been the intellectual architects of our suicidal course."[41] Applying concepts of the marketplace to intellectual life, Friedman argued that the payoff for these "liberals" was support by an entrenched government bureaucracy. In other words, the liberal elite and the government bureaucracy fed off each other. Using a phrase that would be repeated by conservatives throughout the rest of the 20th century, Friedman contended that "the view that government is the problem, not the cure," is hard for the public to understand.[42] According to Friedman's plea, saving the country required a group of intellectuals to give the public an understanding of the importance of the free market.

To undermine the supposed rule of a liberal intelligentsia, Simon urged the business community to support intellectuals who advocated the importance of the free market. Simon called on businesspeople to stop supporting colleges and universities that produced "young collectivists by the thousands" and media "which serve as megaphones for anticapitalist opinion." In both cases, Simon insisted, businesspeople should focus their support on university programs and media that stress procapitalist ideas.[43]

In his call for action, Simon said businesspeople should rush "multimillions to the aid of liberty, in the many places where it is beleaguered." On receiving the largesse of business, he insisted, "Foundations imbued with the philosophy of freedom . . . must take pains to funnel desperately needed funds to scholars, social scientists, writers, and journalists who understand the relationship between political and economic liberty."[44]

In light of Simon's leadership of the John Olin Foundation in the 1970s, it is interesting that two of the leading writers for the free market cause in education, Chester Finn, Jr., and Dinesh D'Souza, are, respectively, John Olin Fellow at the Manhattan Institute and the American Enterprise Institute. Besides supporting scholars at these organizations, the John Olin Foundation backed many conservative causes and, according to one writer, "its pattern of giving became [in the 1970s] more sophisticated and more closely attuned to the potential of grantees for influencing debates on national politics."[45]

Although conservatives talk about the invisible hand of the free market, the trickle-down distribution of ideas is planned using the following methods:

1. Creating foundations and institutes that fund research and policy statements supportive of school choice, privatization of public schools and, more recently, charter schools.
2. Identifying scholars to conduct research, write policy statements and lecture at public forums that are favorable to school choice, privatization of public schools and charter schools.
3. Financing conferences to bring like-minded scholars together for the sharing of ideas and the creation of edited books.
4. Paying scholars to write newspaper opinion pieces that are then distributed to hundreds of newspapers across the country.

This fourth point is an important element in the trickle-down theory of ideas. It is a big leap from writing a research report to being featured on the opinion-editorial page of the *New York Times* or other leading newspapers. It requires connections and a public relations staff to gain quick access to the media. Providing this type of access is one of the important elements in the strategy for spreading a free market agenda. With help from these organizations, I appeared in the 1970s as an "academic expert" on radio and television shows across the country. On one occasion, after the physical exercise portion of an early morning television show, I fielded call-in questions ranging from "Why can't my daughter read?" to "Why are all college professors socialists?" There was never any hint that my appearance on the program resulted from the work of conservative organizations. In the 20th century, this frequently occurred with conservatively backed educational commentators, such as Chester Finn, Jr., and Diane Ravitch. It should be noted that in the 21st century Diane Ravitch became highly critical of the free market education agenda and the drift towards privatization as reflected in her book, *Reign of Error: The Hoax of the Privatization Movement and the Danger to America's Public Schools.*[46]

In *The Transformation of American Politics: The New Washington and the Rise of Think Tanks*, David Ricci described the attempt to mobilize and control public opinion. "Those who talked about developing conservative ideas," Ricci stated, "were committed not just to producing them but to the commercial concept of a product, in the sense of something that, once created, must be placed before the public as effectively as possible."[47]

The Heritage Foundation and the American Enterprise Institute: Marketing School Reform

The Heritage Foundation and the American Enterprise Institute are two of the largest conservative think tanks. They play major roles in shaping the Republican Party's education agenda. Both think tanks fund policy development and disseminate polices and reports to politicians, other policymakers and the general public. They cover a broad range of policy issues from national defense to education. The overwhelming majority of scholars funded by these organizations are considered politically conservative.

In 2016, the Heritage Foundation described itself:

> Founded in 1973, The Heritage Foundation is a research and educational institution—a think tank—whose mission is to formulate and promote conservative public policies based on the principles of free enterprise, limited government, individual freedom, traditional American values, and a strong national defense.[48]

Within the Heritage Foundation is the DeVos Center for Religion and Civil Society.[49] This Center was funded by the Richard and Helen DeVos Foundation, not to be confused with the Dick and Betsy DeVos Family Foundation. The

Richard and Helen DeVos Foundation was created by Richard DeVos, Sr., one of the founders of Amway, and his wife. Reflecting Betsy DeVos's later concerns, Richard DeVos, Sr., created an institute based at Amway headquarters to train teachers on how to integrate free market principles in their courses.[50] These interconnections highlight the linkages between conservative foundations.[51] Reflecting its intellectual debt to Friedrich Hayek, the Heritage Foundation in 2013 offered new members a free copy of Hayek's *Road to Serfdom*.[52]

One of the organizers of the Heritage Foundation, Edwin Fuelner, referred to it as a "secondhand dealer in ideas."[53] The Heritage Foundation developed out of a plan by Pat Buchanan at the request of Republican President Richard Nixon. Shortly after Nixon's 1972 election, Buchanan proposed the creation of an institute that would be a repository of Republican beliefs and would provide a Republican talent bank for conservative thinkers. Buchanan, along with Fuelner and Paul Weyrich, solicited $250,000 in financial support from Joseph Coors, the Colorado brewer and supporter of free market causes. Opening its doors in 1973, the Heritage Foundation received further support from the John Olin Foundation and John Scaife, a Mellon heir and another supporter of conservative causes.[54] After the 1980 election the Heritage Foundation presented President Reagan's White House transition team with a thousand-page volume entitled *Mandate for Change*. The volume, which summarized Republican thinking about a broad range of issues including education, set the tone and direction of the Reagan administration.

Called the General Motors of conservative think tanks, the Heritage Foundation published Chester Finn, Jr., and Diane Ravitch's 1995 report on school reform in their monthly *Policy Review* (again, it should be mentioned, this was before Ravitch rejected the conservative agenda). In the same issue appeared an article by Dinesh D'Souza, the John Olin scholar at the American Enterprise Institute.[55] As described earlier in this book, D'Souza's article, "We the Slaveowners: In Jefferson's America, Were Some Men Not Created Equal?" provided an upbeat note to American slavery.[56]

Reflecting its debt to Friedrich Hayek and its support of school choice plans by the Republican Party, the Heritage Foundation posted on its 2013 website: "Whether through education savings accounts, tax credit scholarship programs, vouchers, online learning, charter schools, or homeschooling, school choice allows access to quality education options that best match individual children's learning needs."[57] Reflecting a free market ideology, the foundation claimed: "School choice options place competitive pressure on public school systems to improve and meet the needs of students. When families have options, public schools must meet the needs of children or risk losing enrollments—and hence dollars—creating a strong incentive for improvement."[58] It listed as the benefits of school choice:

1. Leads to improved academic outcomes;
2. Significantly increases graduation rates;
3. Increases student safety;

4. Improves parental satisfaction with their child's academic and social development and satisfaction with their child's school overall;
5. Introduces competitive pressure on the public education system that lifts all boats, improving outcomes for students who exercise school choice as well as students who remain in public schools; and most importantly,
6. Allows parents to access educational options that meet their child's unique learning needs.[59]

During the 2016 presidential election, the Heritage Foundation supported school choice options. At the state level, they were particularly interested adoption of education savings accounts. The Foundation advocated and described the nature of educational savings accounts as a method for channeling public school money to private choices:

> **Expand Parental Choice in Education by Establishing Education Savings Accounts (ESAs).** States should follow the lead of Arizona, Nevada, Florida, Mississippi, and Tennessee, and establish ESAs. Through ESA options, states deposit a portion of the money that the state would have spent on a child in a public school into a parent-controlled, restricted-use savings account. Parents can then use those dollars to pay for any education-related service, product, or provider, including private school tuition, online learning, special education services and therapies, textbooks, curricula, and college courses, among other education expenditures. Notably, parents can roll over unused funds from year to year to save for anticipated future education-related expenses, such as high school or college tuition.[60]

In addition, the Heritage Foundation advocated turning major federal programs into choice programs: "States should be allowed to make their Title I dollars for low-income children and their Individuals with Disabilities Education Act (IDEA) dollars for children with special needs portable to follow a child to the school of choice—public, private, virtual, or homeschool."[61]

The Heritage Foundation: Choice, Free Markets and Religion

As discussed previously, Republicans believe that, for school choice and free markets to function, individuals must be morally motivated. Reflecting the religious right's influence on the Heritage Foundation and its DeVos Center for Religion and Society, Matthew Spalding at the 25th Annual Resource Bank Meeting of The Heritage Foundation, restated the argument that religion was the basis of American society: "Republican government was possible only if the *private virtues needed for civil society and self-government remained strong and effective.* The civic responsibility and moderation of public passion also requires the *moderation of private passion through the encouragement of individual morality*. And the best way to encourage morality is through the flourishing of religion and the establishment of traditional moral habits [author's emphasis]."[62] He went on to state that the lack of government support of morality was the chief cause of American problems.

> There is a deeper problem as well. Not only does progressive liberalism deny a substantive role for morality in public life, but the extended reach of the state has forced traditional morality—the ground of the old idea of character—into a smaller and smaller private sphere. . . . *If all values are relative, and freedom now means liberation of the human will, it is hard to see any restraints on individual choice* [author's emphasis].[63]

The emphasis on family and religion in the 2016 Republican platform and by the Heritage Foundation can also be found in the Foundation's description of the DeVos Center for Religion and Civil Society:

> The . . . approach to family and religion emphasizes these permanent institutions' role in *sustaining freedom and the common good* [author's emphasis]. We seek to convey the indispensable role of family and religion in our American order and in our conservative philosophy.[64]

Reflecting the Heritage Foundation's emphasis on the family and school choice, the Heritage Foundation published in 2007 *A Parent's Guide to Education Reform*.[65] The goal of the guide was increasing parental control of education through school choice. The guide's major sections are devoted to school choice, including "Why America's Parents Need Greater Choice in Education," "School Choice: A Growing Option in American Education," "Private School Choice" and "Other Forms of School Choice."[66]

After President Trump's election, the Heritage Foundation hosted a meeting with Vice President elect Mike Pence as the keynote speaker at Trump's new international hotel in Washington, DC. Jim DeMint, the Heritage Foundation's president introduced Pence, saying, "I'm trying not to be too giddy tonight" about the election results.[67] *New York Times*' reporter Matt Flegenheimer described the occasion: "On balance, though, the room seemed entirely ready for the Trump age, celebrating the apparent influence of Heritage in Mr. Trump's decision-making thus far and reprising the greatest hits of the 2016 campaign."[68]

American Enterprise Institute: Choice, Free Markets, No Child Left Behind and the Common Core

In contrast to the dissemination role of the Heritage Foundation, the American Enterprise Institute focuses on supporting free market-oriented scholarship. Originally organized in 1943 to educate the public about business, the American

Enterprise Institute dramatically changed in the 1960s under the leadership of William J. Baroody, who applied the concepts of Austrian economics to the world of ideas. Baroody believed there existed a liberal monopoly of ideas. Baroody argued that "a free society can tolerate some degree of concentration in the man ufacture of widgets. But the day it approaches a monopoly in idea formation, that is its death knell."[69]

Baroody proposed a free market of ideas by breaking the liberal monopoly through the establishment of conservative think tanks. Once competition was created, he believed, the invisible hand of the marketplace would determine the value of particular ideas. During the early 1970s, Melvin Laird, Secretary of Defense in the Republican Nixon administration, kicked off a $25 million fund-raising campaign for the American Enterprise Institute in a Pentagon dining room. By the 1980s, the Institute had a staff of 150 and an annual budget of more than $10 million.

The American Enterprise Institute does not emphasize religion in supporting school choice and vouchers. In a posted policy study, it claims: "A survey of the research literature on private school voucher programs shows a consistent pattern. School voucher programs are associated with positive (though small) results for participating students and positive (but also small) results for those students that remain in traditional public schools."[70] The American Enterprise Institute also supported expansion of charter schools as part of their choice agenda. It sponsored an April 6, 2009 conference titled: "Race to the Top? The Promise— and—Challenges of Charter School Growth."[71] The conference was in response to President Obama's efforts to provide more money for charter schools.

In 2016, unlike most conservatives who advocated reducing federal involvement in education, the American Enterprise Institute welcomed an expansion of the federal role using vouchers. The American Enterprise public policy blog, AEIdeas, after the 2016 election of President Donald Trump, posted a commentary, "Uncle Sam and America's schools in the Trump Administration." It argued: "A massive federal choice program could actually end up as the cornerstone of an activist Washington agenda of lots of initiatives. The new administration might reason that what America's education system needs are big, swift, game-changing projects."[72]

What was suggested, similar to Trump's Secretary of Education Betsy DeVos, was turning most federal education programs into vouchers, including "a huge federal pre-school program, a free-college-for-all program, a massive increase in Title I funding, a new federal teacher-pay-raise program, and a federal school-construction program."[73]

Based on President Trump's early pronouncements, the blog assumed that President Trump would invest in schools: "he's expressed interest in a big infrastructure initiative that could include schools. So perhaps the administration is willing to be aggressive on federal education power and pursue a bold agenda-by-items strategy."[74] This would also include a high-quality early childhood program.

"In this scenario," the blog suggested, "lots of progressives might end up pleasantly surprised by a Trump K-12 education agenda."[75]

The Manhattan Institute and the Republican Agenda

The Manhattan Institute's slogan is "Turning Intellect Into Influence" and its stated mission "is to develop and disseminate new ideas that foster greater economic choice and individual responsibility."[76] In 2016 it described itself on its opening page as: "A leading free-market think tank focusing on Economic Growth, Education, Energy and Environment, Health Care, Legal Reform, Public Sector, Race, & Urban Policy."[77] It is a nonprofit organization that funds scholarly work to influence public policy. "The Manhattan Institute," the opening line posted on its 2005 website declares, "has been an important force in shaping American political culture."[78] Even more revealing of its use of scholarship to promote certain political and educational causes is the statement accompanying its plea for donations. Written by the institute's trustee, Walter Wriston, the contribution form states: "The Institute's intellectual capital far exceeds its financial capital, making it the most cost-effective organization of its kind. Although the impact of our ideas dwarfs our financial resources, we still need the latter. There is not a better bargain to be had."[79]

After President Trump announced his choice for U.S. Secretary of Education, Jason Riley, a senior fellow at the Manhattan Institute and columnist for the *Wall Street Journal*, headlined his article "Why Trump's Education Pick Scares Unions." Riley commented:

> Betsy DeVos favors school choice and helped pass Michigan's first charter-school bill. After Donald Trump nominated Betsy DeVos to become education secretary, teachers' union honcho Randi Weingarten tweeted: "Trump has chosen the most ideological, anti-public ed nominee since the creation of the Dept. of Education." Since what's good for the unions is often bad for the schools, and vice versa, Ms. Weingarten's apoplexy is reason to cheer.[80]

Like Secretary DeVos and the 2016 Republican platform, the Manhattan Institute promotes choice and vouchers: "Expansive school choice in the form of vouchers and charter schools is the most attractive option available for improving urban schools. A wide body of evidence accumulated over the last decade shows that school choice helps kids, increases the effectiveness of public schools, and saves taxpayer dollars."[81]

The Manhattan Institute also supports charter schools as an option for children from low-income families.

> Charter schools can dramatically improve the education provided to a city's students. For instance, Stanford University economist Caroline Hoxby argues

that students attending charter schools in New York City performed much better in both math and reading than they would have had they remained in the public schools. The KIPP charter school network, which currently operates charter schools in nineteen states and the District of Columbia, has had phenomenal success improving student proficiency and sending overwhelmingly low-income students to college.[82]

The Institute also supports for-profit education. Writing in the November 21, 2016, issue of *Forbes*, Manhattan Institute Fellow Preston Cooper titled his article: "Public Colleges Aren't a Better Bet Than For-Profits."[83] Reviewing the research on public and for-profit college graduates, Cooper advocates a continuation of for-profit education:

> For-profit colleges must do better, especially given that they are the beneficiaries of billions in taxpayer money. But the idea that public colleges are superior is questionable to say the least. The outgoing Obama administration will doubtless point to the gainful employment data as a mandate to push more students into public colleges' certificate programs, or even make the schools tuition-free. But we should really be concerned about the quality of the career college sector as a whole—public and for-profit schools alike.[84]

The ties between for-profit schools and Republican presidents began as far back 2000 primary when George W. Bush's spoke at the Manhattan Institute during the 2000 primary presidential campaign. At the Institute, Bush was warmly greeted as "my homeboy" by former congressman Reverend Floyd Flake.[85] In this tangled web of connections, Flake had, just before introducing Bush, accepted the headship of the charter school division of the Edison Schools Inc., the largest, at the time, for-profit school-management company in the country.[86]

At the Institute, Bush proposed vouchers for parents of children in failing schools. Similar to the current Secretary of Education Betsy DeVos, he wanted federal Title I funds to be given as vouchers to parents with children in failing schools. This plan was similar to the one praised in a Manhattan Institute's publication about Florida's A-Plus accountability and school choice legislation. These programs operated under the leadership of George W. Bush's brother, Florida's Republican Governor Jeb Bush. The Institute's report, authored by Jay P. Greene, claimed that "By offering vouchers to students at failing schools, the Florida A-Plus choice and accountability system was intended to motivate those schools to improve. . . . This report found that students' academic test scores improve when public schools are faced with the prospect that their students will receive vouchers."[87]

Voucher plans for children from low-income schools was a central focus of the Manhattan Institute's 21st-century education agenda. The institute's research on vouchers is not a search for truth but a search for justifications for its political program. An objective research program would seek to find out if vouchers are an effective means of improving school conditions. However, the institute's program statements indicate a belief that vouchers are the solution: "One of the most important areas of research for our experts will be the need for school vouchers. . . .Vouchers . . . would both improve educational performance and give the existing public school bureaucracy an incentive to make dramatic changes in their schools in order to keep parents satisfied."[88]

A method used by the Institute to promote its education agenda is to pay newspaper reporters to attend so-called informational meetings. The most famous situation occurred in 1996, when both the Manhattan Institute and the American Enterprise Institute, provided research money to Herrnstein and Murray to write *The Bell Curve*, a book that purported to show the intellectual inferiority of lower social classes and African Americans.[89] After the completion of the book, the institute provided honoraria of $500–$1,500 to influential politicians and journalists to attend a seminar on Murray's research.[90]

The Bell Curve exposed what some might consider the inherent racism in some conservative education agendas. Herrnstein and Murray used studies by the Pioneer Fund, which has been criticized because its 1937 founder Wyckliffe Draper supported the eugenics policies of Nazi Germany. After World War II, the Pioneer Fund provided major financial support to psychologist Arthur Jensen and physicist William Shockley, who argued that innate genetic inferiority was the cause of Black poverty and failure in school.[91]

Herrnstein and Murray contended that financial and social elites deserve their social positions because of their superior average IQs. With regard to educational policies, their concern is not with the average student, who they feel receives an adequate education commensurate with his or her IQ, but with the gifted student. In language that suggests intellectual elitism and educational concerns, they contended:

> It needs to be said openly: The people who run the United States—create its jobs, expand its technologies, cure its sick, teach in its universities, administer its cultural and political and legal institutions—are drawn mainly from a thin layer of cognitive ability at the top. . . . It matters enormously not just that the people in the top few centiles of ability get to college . . . or even that many of them go to elite colleges but that they are educated well.[92]

Using this reasoning, Herrnstein and Murray argued for concentrating educational programs on the gifted. Furthermore, in one of the most unusual arguments for school choice, they proposed that the federal government support school choice because parents of gifted children will be the type that will select a tougher academic program. In fact, they argued that because IQ is inherited, educational ambition is primarily "concentrated among the parents of the brightest of the brightest. Policy [referring to school choice] should make it as easy as possible for them to match up with classes that satisfy their ambitions."[93]

In 2008, Charles Murray continued to stress the importance of the inheritance of intelligence in *Real Education: Four Simple Truths for Bringing America's Schools Back to Reality*.[94] Murray argued that college is only suitable for 20 percent of the population with a more realistic number being 10 percent. In 2009, he was asked to present his ideas as part of a panel for the Manhattan Institute's Center for the American University Forum. The Manhattan Institute listed Murray's qualifications as being "W. H. Brady Scholar, American Enterprise Institute."[95] The American Enterprise Institute established the W. H. Brady Program in 2003 and announced at the time:

> AEI [American Enterprise Institute] has established a major new program of research, conferences, student fellowships, and publications concerned with issues of freedom and culture in contemporary society. The W. H. Brady Program in Culture and Freedom has been endowed with a $15 million gift from the W. H. Brady Foundation and from Mr. Brady's daughter, Elizabeth Brady Lurie. The Brady Program will support the work of several AEI scholars, including Charles Murray.[96]

Conclusion

Vouchers and free market theory for public schools was advocated in the 1950s by Milton Friedman, who was influenced by Austrian economist Friedrich Hayek. Since that time certain foundations and think tanks promoted these ideas, such as the Heritage Foundation, the American Enterprise Institute, the Manhattan Institute and the Dick and Betsy DeVos Family Foundation. In 2016, they were given a prominent place in President Donald Trump's administration with its advocacy of vouchers, tuition tax credits, education savings accounts and charter schools.

Free market theory was highlighted by Betsy DeVos's support of unregulated charter schools in Detroit, Michigan. DeVos backed 2010 Michigan legislation expanding the number of charter schools. She helped block legislation that would have kept failing charter schools from expanding or being replicated. In 2016, Secretary DeVos was described as a chief force in defeating Michigan legislation for state standards to identify and close failing charter schools. DeVos's vision was of charter schools opening and closing according to the demands of parental choice in a free market. This free market vision included for-profit schools with 80 percent of Detroit, Flint and Grand Rapids charter schools operating in 2016 as for-profit.[97]

According to *New York Times* reporter Kate Zernike, in defeating Michigan legislation to regulate charter schools, "Ms. DeVos argued that this kind of oversight would create too much bureaucracy and limit choice. A believer in a freer market than even some free market economists would endorse, Ms. DeVos pushed back on any regulation as too much regulation. Charter schools should be allowed to operate as they wish; parents would judge with their feet."[98]

The DeVos-Michigan model of unregulated free market competition between charter schools would, of course, undermine traditional public schools referred to by President Trump as "failing government schools."[99] Tonya Allen, the president of the Skillman Foundation, a nonprofit that works with Detroit children, described DeVos: "She is committed to an ideological stance that is solely about the free market, at the expense of practicality and the basic needs of students in the most destabilized environment in the country."[100] This free market position led Randi Weingarten, the president of the American Federation of Teachers, to call Ms. DeVos "the most ideological, anti-public education nominee" for education secretary since the position was first created in in the 1970s.[101]

As discussed at the chapter's beginning, there is an important religious component to DeVos's advocacy of free market education through charter schools and vouchers. The religious concerns in the Republican education agenda will be discussed in the next chapter. The rhetoric of free market schools often contains the claim of saving poor children from failing public schools—for example, Detroit schools and turning federal Title I funds for students for low-income families into vouchers.

Notes

1 "Republican platform 2016," p. 11. Retrieved from https://gop.com/platform/ on November 23, 2016.

2 Ibid., p. 11.

3 David Brooks, "Bannon versus Trump," *New York Times*, January 10, 2017. Retrieved from www.nytimes.com/2017/01/10/opinion/bannon-versus-trump.html on January 10, 2017.

4 Noam Scheiber, "Betsy DeVos, Trump's Education Pick, Plays Hardball with Her Wealth," *New York Times*, January 9, 2017. Retrieved from www.nytimes.com/2017/01/09/us/politics/betsy-devos-education-secretary.html?ref=todayspaper on January 10, 2017.

5 Nick Tabor and James Walsh, "Government by Gazillionaires: Betsy DeVos," *New York Times*, January 23–February 5, 2017, p. 31.

6 "Republican platform 2016," p. 34.

7 Ibid., p. 33.

8 Holland Christian Schools, "Mission and Beliefs." Retrieved from www.hollandchristian.org/about-us/mission-and-beliefs/ on November 29, 2016.

9 Calvin College, "Who We Are." Retrieved from https://calvin.edu/about/who-we-are/ on November 29, 2016.

10 Kathy Barks Hoffman, "Dick DeVos and Wife Give Millions to Own Foundation," *AP vis Mlive*, April 21, 2006. Retrieved from http://209.157.64.200/focus/f-news/1618311/posts?page=1 on December 11, 2016.

11 Ibid.

12 Dick and Betsy DeVos Family Foundation, "About." Retrieved from www.dbdvfoundation.org/about on December 11, 2016.

13 Trudy Ring, "Trump Picks Right-Wing Activist Betsy DeVos for Secretary of Education," *Advocate*, December 6, 2016. Retrieved from www.advocate.com/politics/2016/11/23/trump-picks-antigay-activist-betsy-devos-secretary-education on December 11, 2016.

14 Northwood University, "About Northwood." Retrieved from www.northwood.edu/about/index.aspx on November 29, 2016.

15 ACCEL, "ACCEL School Locations." Retrieved from https://accelschools.com/schools/ on November 29, 2016.

16 K12, "About Us." Retrieved from www.k12.com/about-k12.html on November 29, 2016.

17 Pansophic Learning, "Safanad and Ron Packard, Founder of K12 Inc., Launch Pansophic Learning and Acquire Assets from K12 to Pursue Global Education Opportunities," June 13, 2014. Retrieved from http://pansophiclearning.com/press_pansophic-launch.html on November 13, 2016.

18 Claire McInerny, "Five Years Later, Indiana's Voucher Program Functions Very Differently," *State Impact: A Reporting Project of WFIU & WTIU with Support from IPBS,* August 19, 2016. Retrieved from http://indianapublicmedia.org/stateimpact/2016/08/19/years-indianas-voucher-program-functions-differently/ on December 1, 2016.

19 Will Drabold, "Here's What Mike Pence Said on LGBT Issues over the Years," *Time,* July 15, 2016. Retrieved from http://time.com/4406337/mike-pence-gay-rights-lgbt-religious-freedom/ on December 1, 2016.

20 For a complete study of the influence of free market theory on education, see Joel Spring, *Economization of Education: Human Capital, Global Corporations, Skill Based Schooling* (New York: Routledge, 2015).

21 Murray N. Rothbard, *Man, Economy, and State: A Treatise of Economic Principles* (Los Angeles, CA: Nash, 1970).

22 See Peter Boettke, "Friedrich A. Hayek (1899–1992)." The Department of Economics, New York University. Retrieved from www.econ.nyu.edu/user/boettke/hayek.htm on August 2, 2000.

23 Friedrich Hayek, *The Road to Serfdom* (Chicago: University of Chicago Press, 1994).

24 Milton Friedman, *Capital and Freedom* (Chicago: University of Chicago Press, 1962), p. 89.

25 Ibid., p. 92.

26 Public Law 107-110, January 8, 2002, "No Child Left Behind Act of 2001," The U.S. Department of Education. Retrieved from www.ed.gov/policy/elsec/leg/esea02/107-110.pdf on February 1, 2009.

27 "No Child Left Behind Act of 2001...," p. 58.

28 Ibid., p. 122.

29 Ibid., pp. 58, 70, 122, 185, 201, 206, 219, 232, 248, 297, 382, 419, 584, 657.

30 James Traub, "Has Benno Schmidt Learned His Lesson?" *New York Times,* October 31, 1994, pp. 51–59.

31 Arthur M. Schlesinger, Jr., *The Disuniting of America* (Knoxville, TN: Whittle Direct Books, 1991), p. 8.

32 Traub, "Has Benno Schmidt Learned His Lesson?"

33 Ibid.

34 Ibid., p. 58.

35 EdisonLearning, "EdisonLearning: Corporate History." Retrieved from www.edisonlearning.com/about_us/corporate_history.be on April 12, 2009.

36 EdisonLearning, "About." Retrieved from http://edisonlearning.com/about-edisonlearning on April 23, 2013.

37 EdisonLearning, "Mission." Retrieved from http://edisonlearning.com/mission.php on December 2, 2016.

38 Ibid.

39 James Smith, *The Idea Brokers and the Rise of the New Policy Elite* (New York: Free Press, 1991), p. 181.

40 William Simon, *A Time for Truth* (New York: Readers Digest Press, 1978), p. 233.

41 Ibid., p. xii.

42 Ibid.

43 Ibid., pp. 232–233.

44 Ibid., p. 230. Smith, *The Idea Brokers* . . ., p. 182.

45 Smith, *The Idea Brokers* . . ., p. 182.

46 Diane Ravitch, *Reign of Error: The Hoax of the Privatization Movement and the Danger to America's Public Schools* (New York: Vintage, 2014).

47 David M. Ricci, *The Transformation of American Politics: The New Washington and the Rise of Think Tanks* (New Haven, CT: Yale University Press, 1993), p. 166.

48 Heritage Foundation, "About." Retrieved from www.heritage.org/about on December 5, 2016.

49 Heritage Foundation, "About, Heritage Teams, DeVos Center for Religion and Civil Society." Retrieved from www.heritage.org/about/staff/departments/devos-center-for-religion-and-civil-society?ac=1 on December 5, 2016.

50 Noam Scheiber, "Betsy DeVos, Trump's Education Pick, Plays Hardball with Her Wealth," *New York Times*, January 9, 2017. Retrieved from www.nytimes.com/2017/01/09/us/politics/betsy-devos-education-secretary.html?ref=todayspaper on January 10, 2017.

51 PewResearch Religion & Public Life Project, "Profile: Heritage Foundation, DeVos Center for Religion and Civil Society." Retrieved from http://projects.pewforum.org/religious-advocacy/heritage-foundation-devos-center-for-religion-and-civil-society/ on December 5, 2016.

52 Heritage Foundation, "Become a Member Today." Retrieved from www.askheritage.org/about on April 23, 2013.

53 Smith, *The Idea Brokers*, p. 197.

54 Ibid., pp. 197–202.

55 Chester E. Finn and Diane Ravitch, "Magna Charter? A Report Card on School Reform in 1995," *Policy Review* (Fall 1995): p. 74; Dinesh D'Souza, "We the Slaveowners: In Jefferson's America, Were Some Men Not Created Equal?" *Policy Review* (Fall 1995): p. 74.

56 D'Souza, "We the Slaveowners."

57 Lindsey M. Burke, ed., "Choosing to Succeed," Heritage Foundation, 2013. Retrieved from www.heritage.org/research/reports/2013/01/choosing-to-succeed-choosing-to-succeed on April 23, 2013.

58 Ibid.

59 Ibid.

60 Heritage Foundation, "Education: Recommendations." Retrieved from http://solutions.heritage.org/culture-society/education/?_ga=1.167443774.1611892490.1480956937 on December 5, 2016.

61 Ibid.

62 Matthew Spalding, "Character and the Destiny of Free Government," in *Building a Culture of Character, Heritage Lectures*, edited by Gregg and Matthew Spalding (Washington, DC: The Heritage Foundation, 2002).

63 Ibid.

64 The Heritage Foundation, DeVos Center for Religion and Civil Society, "About." Retrieved from www.heritage.org/about/staff/departments/devos-center-for-religion-and-civil-society on December 6, 2016.

65 Dan Lips, Jennifer Marshall, and Lindsey Burke, *A Parent's Guide to Education Reform* (Washington, DC: Heritage Foundation, 2007).

66 Ibid., pp. 13–29.

67 Matt Flegenheimer, "Mike Pence Joins Conservatives to Revel in Trump's Win," *The New York Times*, December 6, 2016. Retrieved from www.nytimes.com/2016/12/06/us/politics/mike-pence-heritage-foundation.html?_r=0 on December 8, 2016.

68 Ibid.

69 Quoted in Smith, *The Idea Brokers* . . ., p. 178.

70 Michael Q. McShane, "What Research Tells Us about School Vouchers," Heritage Foundation, February 27, 2013. Retrieved from www.aei.org/speech/education/k-12/what-research-tells-us-about-school-vouchers/ on April 23, 2013.

71 "Race to the Top? The Promise—and—Challenges of Charter School Growth." Retrieved from www.aei.org/events/eventID.1904,filter.all,type.past/event_detail.asp on April 8, 2009.

72 Andy Smarick, "Uncle Sam and America's Schools in the Trump Administration," American Enterprise Institute, December 2, 2013. Retrieved from www.aei.org/publication/k-12-education-trump-administration/ on December 8, 2016.

73 Ibid.

74 Ibid.

75 Ibid.

76 Manhattan Institute for Policy Research, "Home." Retrieved from www.manhattan-institute.org/ on May 6, 2013.

77 Manhattan Institute, "Opening Page." Retrieved from www.manhattan-institute.org/ on December 8, 2016.

78 Manhattan Institute, "About Manhattan Institute." Retrieved from www.manhattan-institute.org/ on January 5, 2005.

79 Manhattan Institute, "Sponsoring the Manhattan Institute." Retrieved from www.manhattan-institute.org/ on January 5, 2005.

80 Jason Riley, "Why Trump's Education Pick Scares Unions," November 30, 2016. Retrieved from www.manhattan-institute.org/ on December 8, 2016.

81 Marcus Winters, "About Urban Education Improving Urban Education: Getting Charter Schools Right, Manhattan Institute." Retrieved from www.manhattan-institute.org/html/csll_urban_education.htm May 6, 2013.

82 Ibid.

83 Preston Cooper, "Public Colleges Aren't a Better Bet than For-Profits," November 21, 2016. Retrieved from www.manhattan-institute.org/html/public-colleges-arent-better-bet-profits-9544.html on December 8, 2016.

84 Ibid.

85 Edward Wyatt, "Floyd Flake to Take Post With Education Company," May 3, 2000. Retrieved from www.nytimes.com on March 29, 2001.

86 Manhattan Institute, "Program Areas: Educational Reform." Retrieved from www.manhattan-institute.org/ on January 5, 2005.

87 Manhattan Institute, "An Evaluation of the Florida A-Plus Accountability and School Choice." Retrieved from www.manhattan-institute.org/ on January 5, 2005.

88 Manhattan Institute, "Program Areas: Educational Reform." Retrieved from www.manhattan-institute.org/ on January 5, 2005.

89 Richard J. Herrnstein and Charles Murray, *The Bell Curve: Intelligence and Class Structure in American Life* (New York: Free Press, 1994).

90 As reported in Michael Lind, *Up from Conservatism: Why the Right Is Wrong for America* (New York: Free Press, 1996), p. 182.

91 Ibid., p. 197.

92 Herrnstein and Murray, *The Bell Curve*, p. 418.

93 Ibid., p. 441.

94 Charles Murray, *Real Education: Four Simple Truths for Bringing America's Schools Back to Reality* (New York: Crown Forum, 2008).

95 Manhattan Institute, Center for the American University Forum: Panel II: "The University of the Future," February 5, 2009. Retrieved from www.manhattan-institute.org/html/mi_recent_events.htm on May 2, 2009.

96 American Enterprise Institute, "AEI Establishes W. H. Brady Program in Culture and Freedom," May 21, 2003. Retrieved from www.aei.org/publications/pubID.17278,filter.social/pub_detail.asp on May 2, 2009.

97 Kate Zernike, "Trump's Education Pick, Has Steered Money from Public Schools," *New York Times*, November 23, 2016. Retrieved from www.nytimes.com/2016/11/23/us/politics/betsy-devos-trumps-education-pick-has-steered-money-from-public-schools.html?ref=todayspaper&_r=0 on December 1, 2016.

98 Kate Zernike, "How Trump's Education Nominee Bent Detroit to Her Will on Charter Schools," *New York Times*, December 12, 2016. Retrieved from www.nytimes.com/2016/12/12/us/politics/betsy-devos-how-trumps-education-nominee-bent-detroit-to-her-will-on-charter-schools.html?rref=collection%2Fsectioncollection%2Fus&action=click&contentCollection=us&region=rank&module=package&version=highlights&contentPlacement=2&pgtype=sectionfront&_r=0 on December 14, 2016.

99 Zernike, "Trump's Education Pick...."

100 Zernike, "How Trump's Education Nominee Bent Detroit...."

101 Zernike, "Trump's Education Pick...."

2

RELIGION AND CULTURE
IN THE REPUBLICAN
EDUCATION AGENDA

In the 2016 Republican platform, religion and immigration received prominent attention. Concerns about immigration included preserving something called traditional American values and ensuring English as the country's dominant language. Drew Westen, in *The Political Brain*, argues that the Republican "master narrative" includes the following beliefs:

- Republicans protect traditional American values.
- Republicans protect traditional religious faith and values.
- Poverty is the result of poor character, and every American has the chance to be financially successful through hard work.
- Republicans protect the free market and rely on the "invisible hand" of the market.
- Republicans protect individual freedom from regulation by big government.[1]

The Preamble to the 2016 Republican platform reflects Westen's description:

> We believe in American exceptionalism.
> We believe the United States of America is
> unlike any other nation on earth.
> We believe America is exceptional because of
> our historic role—first as refuge, then as defender,
> and now as exemplar of liberty for the world to see....
> We believe political freedom and economic
> freedom are indivisible....
> Every time we sing, "God Bless America," we are asking for help. We
> ask for divine help that our country can fulfill its promise. We earn that

help by recommitting ourselves to the ideas and ideals that are the true greatness of America.[2]

In the next section, I will discuss the role of religion in the Republican education agenda and then the issue of culture and language in U.S. schools. An important part of the 2016 Republican agenda was stopping illegal immigration, a controversial issue, as stated in the platform, "That is why we support building a wall along our southern border and protecting all ports of entry." In general, immigration was directly related to the language and culture of schools.

Republican: The Christian Coalition and School Choice

There were three important U.S. Supreme Court decisions that galvanized some religious groups into political action. The first was the 1962 U.S. Supreme Court case *Engel* v. *Vitale*, which denied the official use of prayer in public schools. Since the founding of common schools in the early 19th century, many public schools opened with a prayer and reading from the Protestant Bible. The 1962 decision denied the right of a public school system to conduct official prayer services within school buildings during regular school hours.[3] The second decision was *Abington School District* v. *Schempp* (1963) involving a Pennsylvania law permitting the reading of ten verses from the Bible at the opening of each public school day. Again, the U.S. Supreme Court ruled that this violated the prohibition against government support of religion. Religious texts could be read, the Court argued, as part of an academic course, such as literature or history.[4] As anger swelled over the school prayer and Bible reading decisions, the U.S. Supreme Court added more fuel to the religious concerns with the 1973 decision *Roe v. Wade* legalizing abortion.[5]

Fears of godless classrooms and racial integration after the school prayer and Bible decisions caused a rapid growth of private Christian schools. Like Catholic parents, who thought it unfair to be taxed for support of public schools while they were paying tuition for religious schools, Evangelicals demanded government support of private schools. Initiating a "school choice" movement, Evangelicals argued that state and federal governments should provide financial assistance so that parents could make a choice for their children between public and private schools.[6]

Ralph Reed, a founder of the Christian Coalition and its first executive director, claimed the final straw for evangelical Christians was in the late 1970s when the head of the Internal Revenue Service in the Democratic Carter administration required Christian schools to prove that they were not established to preserve segregation. During the early 1970s, there were rumblings that many of the Christian academies in the South were created as havens for White students fleeing integration. In Reed's words, "More than any other single episode, the IRS move against Christian schools sparked the explosion of the movement that would become known as the religious right."[7] "In this greater moral context," Reed announced, "faith as a political force is not undemocratic; it is the very essence of democracy."[8]

The affiliation of the evangelicals with the Republican Party was explained in a 1996 interview with James Pinkerton, an advisor to the Reagan and Bush administrations and author of *What Comes Next: The End of Big Government— And the New Paradigm Ahead*. In response to a question about divisions within the Republican Party, Pinkerton replied: "Thirty years ago, Kevin Phillips, Pat Buchanan, and people like that were strategizing that we, the Republicans, win over all the southern Fundamentalists and all northern urban Catholics, and we'll build a new American majority party. And that sort of has happened. We won over a lot of urban Catholics and the South is now Republican."[9] Also, William Kristol, editor of the conservative *Weekly Standard*, claimed, "The Republicans made the right bet demographically to bet against Episcopalians, Methodists, and Presbyterians, and with Evangelicals."[10]

The result was a Republican Party divided between those who were primarily interested in issues regarding abortion, morality, culture and schools and those who were primarily interested in economic issues. From the perspective of religiously oriented Republicans, moderate Republicans were concerned with protecting the interests of big business. Reed wanted the Republican Party to become "the party of Main Street, not Wall Street." He went on to claim that "the real battle for the soul of our nation is not fought primarily over the gross national product and the prime interest rate, but over virtues, values, and the culture."[11] Echoing Reed, the political-religious leader Pat Buchanan rejected moderate Republican ties to business and, parodying Calvin Coolidge, said, "The business of America is not business."[12]

One leader of the so-called "electronic church," Jerry Falwell, took the concerns of the religiously oriented conservatives directly to the 1980 Republican presidential candidate, Ronald Reagan. Falwell's television program, "Old-Time Gospel Hour," was seen in more than 12 million homes in the United States. In 1979, before meeting with Reagan, Falwell attended a lunch sponsored by the Heritage Foundation. Its director, Paul Weyrich, told him there was a "moral majority" waiting for a call to political action. Falwell jumped at the phrase and named his group the Moral Majority. Under Falwell's leadership, the organization held rallies around the country supporting the legalization of school prayer, school choice and abolition of abortion. Within a space of 2 years, the Moral Majority had 2 million members and was raising $10 million annually.[13]

The wedding between Ronald Reagan and the Moral Majority occurred shortly after the 1980 Republican convention when Reagan was asked to address 20,000 Evangelicals at a rally in Dallas. Reagan told the group, "I know that you cannot endorse me [because of the tax-exempt status of the Moral Majority], but I endorse you and everything you do."[14] Giving hope to Evangelicals opposed to evolutionary theory, Reagan expressed doubts about the plausibility of Darwinian ideas. After the 1980 election, Reagan supported the religious right's agenda by endorsing legislation for a tuition tax credit to allow parents to choose between public and private schools and by promising to support a school prayer amendment to the U.S. Constitution. After 1980, school choice and school prayer became a standard fixture in Republican platforms.

By 1996, the political power of evangelical Christians was mainly expressed through the Christian Coalition. For instance, Republican presidential candidate Bob Dole wanted to focus on an economic agenda while avoiding a strong stand against abortion, but the Christian Coalition threatened to disrupt the 1996 convention unless the party platform opposed abortion. It included in the 1996 Republican platform: "The unborn has a fundamental individual right to life which cannot be infringed. We support a human life amendment to the Constitution and we endorse legislation to make clear that the Fourteenth Amendment's protections apply to unborn children."[15] Campaigns to limit or eliminate legal abortion continued into the 2016 election.

Abandoning efforts at a constitutional amendment allowing for school prayer, as I explain later in this chapter, the 2016 Republican platform stated: "We support the public display of the Ten Commandments as a reflection of our history and our country's Judeo-Christian heritage and further affirm the rights of religious students to engage in voluntary prayer at public school events and to have equal access to school facilities. We assert the First Amendment right of freedom of association for religious, private, service, and youth organizations to set their own membership standards."[16]

Christian Coalition: Religious Politics

The Christian Coalition is the leading political advocacy group for evangelical Christians. In 2016, the Christian Coalition described itself as: "a political organization, made up of pro-family Americans who care deeply about ensuring that government serves to strengthen and preserve, rather than threaten, our families and our values. To that end, we work continuously to identify, educate and mobilize Christians for effective political action."[17] The stated mission of the organization is:

- **Represent** the pro-family point of view before local councils, school boards, state legislatures and Congress
- **Speak out** in the public arena and in the media
- **Train** leaders for effective social and political action
- **Inform** pro-family voters about timely issues and legislation
- **Protest** anti-Christian bigotry and defend the rights of people of faith[18]

The Christian Coalition was organized in 1989 by televangelist Pat Robertson and Ralph Reed after Pat Robertson's unsuccessful presidential campaign in

1988. Its headquarters is in Washington, DC, where it can maintain close tabs on federal legislation. It immediately alerts its membership about any bill in Congress that is important to the interests of its members. Members are given the postal and e-mail addresses and the fax and telephones numbers of their Congressional representatives so that they can express their viewpoints on pending legislation. However, the real political activity is in local churches. This raises the issue of religious involvement in politics.

In 2004, the Christian Coalition provided the following justification for blending religion and politics. The organization's 2004 website stated,

> We are driven by the belief that people of faith have a right and a responsibility to be involved in the world around them. That involvement includes community, social and political action. Whether on a stump, in print, over the airways the Christian Coalition is dedicated to equipping and educating God's people with the resources and information to battle against anti-family legislation.[19]

In 2016, the Christian Coalition called for members to participate in political action:

Take Action

See our recent Action Alerts

[1] Find out what issues we're working on now and how you can help.
[2] Participate in one of our campaigns
[3] Check out our most recent petitions and lobbying campaigns. Participate and spread the word!
[4] Contact your elected officials. Your elected officials need to hear from you on a regular basis. Make sure they do!
[5] Speak out in the public arena: Don't be silent when it comes to your values! Find out more about how to be heard in your community.
[6] Citizenship Sunday: Hold A Voter Registration Drive at Your Church.
[7] Spread the word: Let others know about content you find in our site. Forward messages and post on other websites.[20]

The Christian Coalition issues voter guides described in 2016: "These voter guides are issued Christian Coalition Voter Guides provide voters with critical information about where candidates stand on important faith and family issues."[21]

Voter guides distributed through churches threaten their tax-exempt status. Therefore, the Christian Coalition provides a carefully crafted list of dos and don'ts. In the official words of the organization, "And although a church's tax status does limit the amount of political activity it may engage in, it does not prohibit a church from encouraging citizenship."[22] The Christian Coalition informs ministers that the provided list of "do's and don'ts will help guide you, without jeopardizing your church's tax-exempt status, as you lead your congregation into the God-given duties of citizenship. Remember, as Edmund Burke warned, 'All that is necessary for the triumph of evil is for good men to do nothing.'"[23]

The Christian Coalitions' list of permissible political actions by churches provides an actual guide to the methods ministers can use to influence their congregations. The Christian Coalition provides ministers with the following instructions:

What Churches May Do

Conduct non-partisan voter registration drives

Distribute non-partisan voter education materials, such as Christian Coalition voter guides and scorecards

Host candidate or issue forums where all viable candidates are invited and allowed to speak

Allow candidates and elected officials to speak at church services; if one is allowed to speak, others should not be prohibited from speaking

Educate members about pending legislation

Lobby for legislation and may spend no more than an insubstantial amount of its budget (five percent is safe) on direct lobbying activities

Endorse candidates in their capacity as private citizens—A pastor does not lose his right to free speech because he is an employee of a church

Participate fully in political committees that are independent of the church

The Christian Coalition also provides boundaries for the political action of churches:

What Churches May Not Do

Endorse candidates directly or indirectly from the pulpit on behalf of the church

Contribute funds or services (such as mailing lists or office equipment) directly to candidates or political committees

Distribute materials that clearly favor any one candidate or political party

Pay fees for partisan political events from church funds

Allow candidates to solicit funds while speaking in church

Set up a political committee that would contribute funds to political candidates[24]

The Christian Coalition joined hands with major conservative think tanks to support the Republican education agenda. Many of its education goals appear in No Child Left Behind. No Child Left Behind contains many items dear to heart of Christian conservatives, including support of abstinence education, protection of school prayer, public funding of faith-based organizations, the Boy Scouts of America Equal Access Act and control of Internet and other forms of pornography. The Christian Coalition along with conservative think tanks played an important role in selling No Child Left Behind to politicians and the public.

No Child Left Behind and Religion

Religious advocates were able to include their concerns about school prayers and government funding of faith-based organizations in the 2001 federal legislation No Child Left Behind. No Child Left Behind was a renewal of Title I of the 1965 Elementary and Secondary Education Act (ESEA). Title I of ESEA, signed by President Johnson on April 11, 1965, No Child Left Behind opens, "TITLE I—IMPROVING THE ACADEMIC ACHIEVEMENT OF THE DISADVANTAGED."[25]

Religious groups were able to infuse their ideas in the legislation as part of a compromise between Republicans and Democrats. No Child Left Behind contained the provisions for creating curriculum standards and accountability through standardized testing. An important difference with the 1965 Title I, which targeted students from low-income families, was that No Child Left Behind all included all students in its testing and curriculum standards provisions.

What concerns of religious-oriented Republicans are expressed in No Child Left Behind? First, No Child Left Behind supported public funding of faith-based organizations. In July, 2004, the U.S. Department of Education issued a pamphlet describing the relationship between No Child Left Behind and faith-based organizations. The pamphlet asserted, "With No Child Left Behind, schools and religious organizations can become even more powerful allies in the effort to ensure that all children—regardless of their race, family income or the language spoken in their homes—receive a high-quality education."[26] The pamphlet described the following opportunities for faith-based organizations to participate in No Child Left Behind:

> Faith-based organizations can receive funds to provide tutoring and other academic enrichment services for eligible low-income students. Religious organizations can become supplemental educational services providers by applying to states and then working with districts to provide services directly to students in reading, language arts and mathematics.[27]

In addition to becoming supplemental educational services providers, faith-based groups can receive grants from a range of other programs that provide extra academic help.

President George W. Bush's Secretary of Education Rod Paige promoted government funding of faith-based organizations. Standing in front of a poster proclaiming "Compassion in Action" at the 2004 11th Regional White House

Conference on Faith-Based and Community Initiatives, Secretary Paige declared, "With a stroke of a pen, the President signaled that this Administration will knock down any barrier, will do whatever it takes to get people of faith and goodwill involved in helping solve some of the problems in our society."[28] When John Porter was appointed U.S. Department of Education's Director of Faith-Based and Community Initiative, Secretary Paige described him thus: "John Porter is a leader in our nation's army of compassion. Some of the most successful, uplifting and effective programs to help children are run by faith-based and community organizations. We plan to utilize the hundreds of faith-based and community soldiers around the country to ensure that every child of every religion, race and ethnicity gets the best education America can offer them, and John will help guide our efforts."[29]

Religious-oriented Republicans linked poverty to a failure in individual character and values in contrast to economic conditions. Consequently, No Child Left Behind contained programs for character education. "Character education," according to a press release from the U.S. Department of Education, "is a key feature of No Child Left Behind, the landmark education reform law designed to change the culture of American schools."[30]

No Child Left Behind also linked, similar to President's Trump Secretary of Education Betsy DeVos, character education to democracy and free markets. The legislation's "Section 2345: Cooperative Civic Education and Economic Education" supports research to determine the "effects of educational programs on students' development of the knowledge, skills, and *traits of character essential* for the preservation and *improvement of constitutional democracy*; and . . . effective participation in, and the preservation and improvement of, *an efficient market economy* [author's emphasis].[31]

As explained in Chapter 1, many Republicans believed a free market required citizens infused with moral values. Section 5431 of No Child Left Behind called for "Partnerships in Character Education Program" to support "the design and implementation of character education programs that . . . are able to be integrated into classroom instruction and to be consistent with State academic content standards."[32] This section of the legislation even listed possible elements of character education instruction; this may be the first time in history where federal legislation actually identified elements of character considered important for the functioning of American society. The legislation provides the following examples:

(A) Caring.
(B) Civic virtue and citizenship.
(C) Justice and fairness.
(D) Respect.
(E) Responsibility.
(F) Trustworthiness.
(G) Giving.[33]

In 2002, the U.S. Department of Education began funding applications for character education programs under the No Child Left Behind Act. U.S. Secretary of Education Rod Paige announced in 2003, "We have invested nearly $24 million in character education in FY 2003 because we believe that building strong character is as essential as reading, math and science."[34] However, the results were disappointing. In 2007, the U.S Secretary of Education released a report. According to *Education Week* reporter Debra Viadero, "After reviewing the research on 41 programs aimed at instilling character in students, the U.S. Department of Education gave 'positive' ratings to just two of them and rated seven more as 'potentially positive.'"[35]

No Child Left Behind and School Prayer

The Christian Coalition and other groups had pressed unsuccessfully for a constitutional amendment allowing school prayer and Bible reading. Realizing the futility of achieving a constitutional amendment, religious groups accepted a compromise provision in the No Child Left Behind legislation. The legislation's "Section 9524: School Prayer" commands:

> The Secretary [U.S. Secretary of Education] shall provide and revise guidance, not later than September 1, 2002, and of every second year thereafter, to State educational agencies, local educational agencies, and the public on *constitutionally protected prayer* in public elementary schools and secondary schools, including making the guidance available on the Internet.[36]

This provision did not satisfy those who wanted choice of religious schools, because they believed public schools were inherently anti-religious and taught secular humanism. Secular humanism is defined as dependence on human reason in contrast to faith in God to guide for ethical decisions. Without God in the school, the some evangelicals believe, the school teaches secular humanism. An important court case involving secular humanism began in 1983 in the schools of Hawkins County, Tennessee, when a local parent expressed concern about a new series of readers published by Holt, Rinehart & Winston. According to the complaint, the books were filled with "minorities, foreigners, environmentalism, women in nontraditional roles, and open-ended value judgments without clear right and wrong answers."[37]

There was criticism of a wide range of topics under the banner of secular humanism. Believing that unregulated capitalism was God's will, critics objected to suggestions of environmentalism because it led to government intervention in the economy. Protestors objected to teaching religious tolerance because it suggested that other religions were equal in value to Christianity. The teaching of international cooperation, evangelicals argued, could lead to world government, which would mean the reign in their eyes of the antichrist. They also objected to stories that suggested humane treatment of animals and vegetarianism because

God created animals for human use and exploitation. Evangelicals particularly objected to any story suggesting that hunting was wrong. Also, they felt that stories suggesting the depletion of resources and the extinction of species were denying God's promise to meet all human needs. Men and women portrayed in nontraditional roles would, according to protestors, destroy the traditional Christian family in which wives remained at home raising their children. For this reason, they opposed anything that smacked of feminism.[38]

After 4 years of litigation, the Sixth Circuit Court of Appeals ruled that public schools did not have to accommodate religious objections to the Holt, Rinehart & Winston readers. A previous lower court ruling suggested that religious objections to the books could be accommodated by assigning different texts or by teaching reading at home. The final ruling enhanced the power of school boards by requiring children attending public schools to read the books selected by school officials.[39]

In 1987, the National Legal Foundation, affiliated with Pat Robertson's Christian Broadcasting Network, supported an Alabama case against public schools teaching secular humanism. Robertson used his television show, *The 700 Club*, to publicize the case as a Christian battle against the anti-religious tenets of secular humanism. People for the American Way and the American Civil Liberties Union provided legal opposition to the work of the National Legal Foundation. The case received a great deal of attention when Robertson announced his candidacy for the Presidency in 1988.[40]

The plaintiffs charged that forty-five textbooks approved for Alabama schools taught secular humanism. Supporting their case was a consent decree signed by Alabama's Governor George Wallace stating that the religion of secular humanism should be excluded from Alabama schools. On *The 700 Club*, Robertson quoted former Alabama governor and pro-segregationist George Wallace, "I don't want to teach ungodly humanism in the schools where I'm governor." In turn, Robertson declared that taking secular humanism out of the schools was an issue of "religious freedom."[41]

The primary legal problem for the plaintiffs was proving that secular humanism was a religion. Again, the issue was about textbooks teaching children that they could make their own moral decisions without relying on the Word of God. In a lower court decision, religious conservative Judge Brevard Hand ruled that secular humanism was indeed a religion and that the use of books espousing secular humanism should be removed from the schools. This decision was reversed by the Eleventh Circuit Court of Appeals, which ruled that the books did not violate the First Amendment: "Rather the message conveyed is one of a governmental attempt to instill in Alabama public school children such values as independent thought, tolerance of diverse views, self-respect, maturity, self-reliance, and logical decision-making. This is an entirely appropriate secular effect."[42]

In 1994, after failing to counter secular humanism and achieve a school prayer amendment, the Christian Coalition decided to make what Reed called a "seismic shift" in strategy. Rather than campaigning for school prayer, the decision was made to adopt Robertson's language and support an amendment for religious freedom. Reed argued that an emphasis on religious freedom as opposed to the narrower issue of school prayer would appeal to a broader religious audience. The religious freedom amendment would guarantee the right of religious expression to all people in all public settings.[43] In 1996, reflecting what was now becoming a compromise position about school prayer, Haley Barbour, Chairman of the National Republican Committee, stated that the Republican Party supported the "right to voluntary prayer in schools . . . whether through a constitutional amendment or through legislation, or a combination of both."[44]

Leaders of the Christian Coalition hoped that a religious freedom amendment would protect the rights of students to express their religious beliefs in the classroom. For example, it was believed that a student should have the right to support creationism over evolutionary theory in science classes. In supporting the religious freedom amendment Reed described the case of a Tennessee high school student, Brittney Settle, who was failed for turning in an essay on the life of Jesus Christ. Without citing the details of the case, Reed claimed that a federal court upheld the right of the school to flunk the student for her religious beliefs. In reaction to the case, Reed stated, "A religious freedom amendment would protect her, along with unbelieving students who are nervous about being compelled to participate in mandatory religious exercises in public schools."[45]

Republican Representatives Newt Gingrich and Dick Armey promised the Christian Coalition that for its support of Republican candidates they would introduce a proposal for inclusion of religious freedom in the First Amendment. The proposed changes to the First Amendment would "protect religious freedom, including the right of students in public schools to pray without government sponsorship or compulsion." In addition, the changes would prohibit state and federal governments from denying anyone "equal access to a benefit, or otherwise discriminate against any person, on account of religious belief, expression, or exercise."[46]

During the hearings, Republican Representative Henry Hyde, the head of the House Judiciary Committee, complained that public school teachers often discriminated against Christians by denying reports and essays on Jesus Christ. "Public school teachers, who accept reports on witches," Hyde explained, "[and] forbid students from writing reports on Jesus. This is madness."[47] One cynical critic, David Ramage, Jr., president emeritus of the McCormick Theological Seminary, accused the Christian Coalition of wanting to rush the amendments through the House of Representatives so that House members' positions could be included in their fall voting guide. Voting "no" on the religious freedom changes, Ramage suggested, would be listed in the Christian Coalition's voter guide as "a vote against religious freedom" or a "vote against God."[48]

Unable to achieve an amendment to the U.S. Constitution, No Child Left Behind was seen as an opportunity to protect religious freedom. The school prayer section of No Child Left Behind mandated the protection of religious freedom in public schools. The legislation required the U.S. Secretary of Education to issue guidance for protecting constitutionally approved prayer. Dated February 7, 2003, the U.S. Department of Education guide reminded local education agencies that they must report that their schools have "no policy that prevents, or otherwise denies participation in, constitutionally protected prayer in public schools as set forth in this guidance."[49]

The guidelines stated, "Although the Constitution forbids public school officials from directing or favoring prayer," students do not "shed their constitutional rights to freedom of speech or expression at the schoolhouse gate," and the Supreme Court has made clear that "private religious speech, far from being a First Amendment orphan, is as fully protected under the Free Speech Clause as secular private expression." Moreover, not all religious speech that takes place in the public schools or at school-sponsored events is governmental speech. For example, "nothing in the Constitution . . . prohibits any public school student from voluntarily praying at any time before, during, or after the school day," and students may pray with fellow students during the school day on the same terms and conditions that they may engage in other conversation or speech. Likewise, local school authorities possess substantial discretion to impose rules of order and pedagogical restrictions on student activities, but they may not structure or administer such rules to discriminate against student prayer or religious speech.[50]

The 2008 Republican platform restated the No Child Left Behind support of religious freedom in public schools: "We will energetically assert the right of students to engage in voluntary prayer in schools and to have equal access to school facilities for religious purposes."[51] The 2012 Republican platform reiterated its support of school prayer and public display of religious messages: "We support the public display of the Ten Commandments as a reflection of our history and of our country's Judeo-Christian heritage, and we affirm the right of students to engage in prayer at public school events in public schools and to have equal access to public schools and other public facilities to accommodate religious freedom in the public square."[52]

In summary, the school prayer and faith-based provisions of No Child Left Behind did not satisfy those who considered public schools as teaching secular humanism. Consequently, there would continue to be an effort to achieve vouchers that would allow parents to send their children to private religious schools. In 2017, Secretary of Education Betsy DeVos represented this concern as reflected in her life's work described in Chapter 1.

The Culture Wars

Traditionally, Republicans were concerned with maintaining something called "American culture" and making English the U.S.'s official language. While the opening of the 2016 Republican platform, as previously quoted, emphasizes

American exceptionalism and patriotism, there is nothing in the platform about schools teaching American values. In part, this is a result of the Republican rejection of federal or state-imposed curriculum standards that would interfere in free competition between schools using vouchers. However, the teaching of American values and culture has been a traditional Republican concern along with maintaining English as the language of schooling. This appears in the 2016 Republican platform: "To ensure that all students have access to the mainstream of American life, we support the English First approach and oppose divisive programs that limit students' ability to advance in American society."[53]

During Republican Ronald Reagan's presidency in the 1980s, Republicans began to speak out against multiculturalism and forms of bilingual education designed to maintain minority languages and cultures. It was Republican President Reagan's Secretary of Education William Bennett who voiced the strongest objections to multiculturalism, which he felt was undermining American values. In 1986, Bennett made a name for himself in academic circles when he launched a public attack against the Stanford University faculty for replacing a freshman undergraduate course entitled "Western Culture," encompassing fifteen works in Western philosophy and literature, with a course entitled "Cultures, Ideas, and Values," with books by "women, minorities, and persons of color."[54] Bennett argued that students should be required to study Western culture because it provided the framework for American government and culture. In addition, he stated, "Probably most difficult for the critics of Western culture to acknowledge is that 'the West is good.'" Western culture, according to Bennett, has "set the moral, political, economic, and social standards for the rest of the world."[55]

Bennett blamed the "liberal elite," a code phrase for culturally influential Democrats, for the advancement of multiculturalism and the undermining of traditional American values. Bennett argued that the culture wars were between the beliefs held by most citizens and "the beliefs of a liberal elite that today dominates many of our institutions and who therefore exert influence on American life and culture."[56] This liberal elite, according to Bennett, inhabited universities, the literary and artistic worlds; liberal religious institutions; and the media. The liberal elite, Bennett contended, was different from former bourgeois elites, who valued the importance of the family, public morality, hard work and individual entrepreneurship. In contrast, the liberal elite rejected many traditional Christian values and looked with scorn on Americans who believe in the value of hard work and economic individualism. Furthermore, this liberal elite supported ideas that were an anathema to the religiously oriented Republicans, such as multiculturalism, sexual freedom and gay and lesbian relationships.

Another Reagan appointee Lynne Cheney, the wife of the future Republican Vice President Dick Cheney, shared with William Bennett a similar philosophy about the humanities. President Reagan made Cheney the head of the National Endowment for the Humanities where she served from 1986 to 1993. This gave her an important role in influencing research and writing about American culture and specifically about American history. In September 1987, Cheney issued "American Memory: A Report on the Humanities in the Nation's Public Schools."[57] In the report she criticized history instruction in public schools: "Long relied upon to transmit knowledge of the past to upcoming generations, our schools today appear to be about a different task. Instead of preserving the past, they more often disregard it, sometimes in the name of 'progress'—the idea that today has little to learn from yesterday."[58]

She criticized the emphasis on social studies in contrast to teaching individual disciplines, such as history, political science, economics and geography. "The culprit is 'process,'" Cheney wrote, "the belief that we can teach them how to understand the world in which they live without conveying to them the events and ideas that have brought it into existence." In her conclusion, she warned, "we run the danger of unwittingly proscribing our own heritage."[59]

The 1996 Republican platform offered a specific remedy for those fearing a loss of traditional American culture: "To reinforce our American heritage, we believe our nation's Governors, State legislators, and local school boards should support requiring our public schools to dedicate one full day each year solely to studying the Declaration of Independence and the Constitution."[60] The platform criticized Democratic President Bill Clinton for not limiting bilingual education to being solely a method for learning English, stated: "We condemn Bill Clinton's refusal, once again, to protect and preserve the most precious symbol of our Republic. English, our common language, provides a shared foundation which has allowed people from every corner of the world to come together to build the American nation."[61]

During the 1996 campaign Republican candidate Bob Dole said: "For more than two centuries now, English has been a force for unity, indispensable to the process of transforming untold millions of immigrants from all parts of the globe into citizens of the most open and free society the world has ever seen."[62] Specifically emphasizing bilingual education as a method to be used only for learning English, the 1996 Republican platform related the bilingual issue to making English the official U.S. language: "For newcomers, learning the English language has always been the fastest route to the mainstream of American life. That should be the goal of bilingual education programs. We support the official recognition of English as the nation's common language."[63]

In the 2000 presidential campaign, future Republican President George W. Bush advocated cultural unity and opposed bilingual education. Bilingual education had become a symbol for a multicultural society. Also, there was concern about patriotism and flag worship, particularly with reported incidents of flag burning. The 2000 Republican platform called for cultural unity and protection of the national flag: "Our country's ethnic diversity within a shared national culture is unique in all the world. We benefit from our differences, but we must also strengthen the ties that bind us to one another. Foremost among those is the flag. Its deliberate desecration is not 'free speech' but an assault against both our proud history and our greatest hopes."[64]

The 2008 Republican platform, as did the 2012 platform, continued stressing English as a culturally unifying language. The 2008 platform stated, "Another sign of our unity is the role of English as our common language. It has enabled people from every corner of the world to come together to build this nation. For newcomers, it has always been the fastest route to the mainstream of American life. English empowers."[65] And the platform emphasized, "That is why fluency in *English must be the goal of bilingual education programs.* We support the recognition of English as the nation's common language [author's emphasis]."[66]

Standards and Tests: The Politics of Culture

Protecting traditional American values became an issue with the creation of academic standards for history and the content for standardized history tests. In the development of national standards and tests in the 1990s, history proved to be the most politically contentious subject. Because history is shaped by and contains political values, the debate over history standards reflects broad divisions in political ideas. In 1986, foreshadowing the national standards debate over history, California Superintendent of Public Instruction Bill Honig appointed Diane Ravitch, who at the time was an adjunct professor at Teachers College, Columbia University, and Charlotte Crabtree, a professor of education at UCLA, to a panel to rewrite the state social studies curriculum. Ravitch would later be appointed in 1991 by President George H. W. Bush as Assistant Secretary of Education and Counselor to Secretary of Education Lamar Alexander. After her appointment to the U.S. Department of Education, Ravitch promoted "the creation of academic standards."[67]

In 1987, California officials approved a framework for the teaching of history that was primarily written by Ravitch and Crabtree.[68] The controversy was about the California framework, which centered on its portrayal of the United States as a land of immigrants. The debate also occurred in New York with Arthur Schlesinger, Jr., and Diane Ravitch playing a major role.[69] The dispute highlights significant differences regarding the teaching and interpretation of U.S. history. For socially conservative Republicans, the major purpose in public school history instruction was creating national unity by teaching a common set of political and social values. These common values, according to this conservative approach, should be a reflection of the beliefs underlying American institutions. In Arthur Schlesinger's words, "For better or worse, the White Anglo-Saxon Protestant tradition was for two centuries, and in crucial respects still is, the dominant influence on American culture and society. . . . The language of the new nation, its laws, its institutions, its political ideas, its literature, its customs, its precepts, its prayers, primarily derived from Britain."[70]

From a Republican perspective, the teaching of core values would help reduce racial and ethnic strife and ensure the perpetuation of traditional American values. Within this framework, the content of U.S. history should emphasize the common struggles and benefits received from U.S. institutions by the diverse cultural groups composing its population. The study of differing cultures in the United States, such as Native American and African, should emphasize tolerance and unity under common institutions.

An objection to the California framework came from Nathan Huggins, a Harvard professor of African American studies and history at Harvard. Huggins warned, "A stress on 'common culture' turns history into a tool of national unity, mandated principally by those anxious about national order and coherence."[71] There was outrage among some African Americans, Mexican Americans and Native Americans at the concept of the United States being a land of immigrants. All three groups could claim to be unwilling members of U.S. society who were forced into participation by slavery and conquest. From this perspective, the history of the United States was marked by White violence against Africans, Mexicans, Asians and Native Americans.

Stanford University Professor of African and Afro-American studies Sylvia Wynter argued that the California history framework "does not move outside the conceptual field of our present essentially Euro American cultural model."[72] The framework, she argued, did not provide a means for understanding the plight of minority groups in the United States. Wynter asked, "How did the dispossession of the indigenous peoples, their subordination, and the mass enslavement of the people of Black African descent come to seem 'just and virtuous' actions to those who affected them? How does the continuance of this initial dispossession, in the jobless, alcohol ridden reservations, the jobless drug and crime ridden inner cities . . . still come to seem to all of us, as just, or at the very least, to be in the nature of things?"[73]

Joyce King, then a Santa Clara University education professor and one of the leading critics of the California framework, was particularly disturbed by the "we are all immigrants" interpretation of U.S. history. King called this approach "dysconscious racism . . . an impaired consciousness or a distorted way of thinking about race . . . [that] tacitly accepts dominant White norms and privileges."[74] The California framework, she argued, presented a triumphant chronological history progressing to an inevitable point when all groups are able to acquire the supposed "superior" values of White Anglo-Saxon society. In this context, national unity required that all cultural groups recognize the advantages of White Anglo-Saxon traditions.

In their 1996 campaign book, Republican candidates Bob Dole and Jack Kemp joined the chorus demanding a more upbeat American history be taught in public schools. Dole and Kemp declared: "Where schools should instill an appreciation of our country and its history, often they seem to reflect a blindness toward America and its finer moments."[75]

Dinesh D'Souza, a John Olin scholar at the American Enterprise Institute, published in 1991 *Illiberal Education: The Politics of Race and Sex on Campus* criticizing affirmative action and multicultural education.[76] The research and writing for the book was supported by the conservative American Enterprise Institute and John Olin Foundation. Attacking the supposed domination of politically correct thinking on American college campuses, D'Souza argued that affirmative action was destructive of minority students and the quality of education. Affirmative action, he argued, results in colleges admitting many poorly prepared minority students. "The consequence," he claimed, was "minority students placed in 'high risk' intellectual environments where they compete against vastly better-prepared students, and where their probability of graduation is known to be low."[77] D'Souza argued that multiculturalism and feminism were destroying liberal education through the replacement in college courses of significant books written by White males with inferior books written by minorities and women.

No Child Left Behind and the Common Core State Standards: The End of Multiculturalism and Linguistic Diversity

No Child Left Behind required states to standardize their curricula, which, essentially, eliminated the possibility of public school curricula reflecting the culture of the students they served. The Common Core State Standards had the same effect. They were issued in 2010 by the National Governors Association and states could voluntarily adopt them. It is important to note that the 2016 Republican platform specifically rejected the Common Core State Standards as a hindrance to a free market of school choice where schools might reflect a variety of curricula.

The 2016 Republican platform states: "We likewise repeat our longstanding opposition to the imposition of national standards and assessments, encourage the parents and educators who are implementing alternatives to Common Core, and congratulate the states which have successfully repealed it."[78] This statement is followed by a statement on school choice: "Their [parents] education reform movement calls for choice-based, parent-driven accountability at every stage of schooling."[79]

The 2016 Republican commitment to school choice and free markets for schools was a major change from previous concerns about multiculturalism and linguistic diversity. For instance, unregulated charter schools, exemplified by Secretary of Education Betsy DeVos's work in Detroit, would allow for parents to choose between schools reflecting a variety of cultures and using a variety of languages in the classroom.

Changes in Republican attitudes as a result of a commitment to vouchers and a free market for schools can be traced from No Child Left Behind. No Child Left Behind favored a monolingual and monocultural society as opposed to a multilingual and pluralistic society. The legislation erased the efforts to institute bilingual education designed to maintain family languages. The efforts to create multicultural school systems were defeated as the new law mandated standardized tests and state standards to regulate the school curriculum to ensure that a single culture would dominate the schools.

In 2001, Republican President George W. Bush and a majority of Congress opposed bilingual education and stood firmly for the principle that the primary objective of U.S. schools should be teaching English without maintaining minority languages. Reflecting the ongoing culture wars, No Child Left Behind placed the federal government's support on the side of English acquisition, not bilingual education. The part of the legislation titled "English Language Acquisition, Language Enhancement, and Academic Act" changed the name of the federal government's Office of Bilingual Education to "Office of English Language Acquisition, Language Enhancement, and Academic Achievement for Limited English Proficient"; its shortened name was simply "Office of English Language Acquisition." The director of bilingual education and minority languages affairs became the director of English language acquisition.[80]

Limited exception to English acquisition was provided for Native Americans and Puerto Ricans. While recognizing programs designed to maintain Native American languages and Spanish, the law mandated that the major purpose was English proficiency. The legislation authorized programs, serving Native American (including Native American Pacific Islander) children and children in the Commonwealth of Puerto Rico, "designed for Native American children learning and studying Native American languages and children of limited Spanish proficiency, except that an outcome of programs serving such children *shall be increased English proficiency among such children* [author's emphasis]."[81]

Specifically targeted for rejection by Republicans in 2016, Common Core State Standards issued by the National Governors Association in 2010 were to prepare students to enter a global workforce: "[The Common Core State Standards] are informed by other top performing countries, so that all students are prepared to succeed in our global economy and society." These standards define the knowledge and skills students should have within their K-12 education careers so that they will graduate high school able to succeed in entry-level, credit-bearing academic college courses and in workforce training programs.[82] The standards:

- Are aligned with college and work expectations;
- Are clear, understandable and consistent;
- Include rigorous content and application of knowledge through high-order skills;
- Build upon strengths and lessons of current state standards;
- Are informed by other top performing countries, so that all students are prepared to succeed in our global economy and society; and
- Are evidence-based.[83]

Focused on job preparation for a global workforce, the standards gave little emphasis to multiculturalism. The only global reading mandated by the standards are "myths and stories from around the world" without any suggestion that students might read foreign novels or collections of short stories. Primarily focusing on teaching skills, the Standards for Reading state:

> The standards mandate certain critical types of content for all students, including classic myths and stories from around the world, foundational U.S. documents, seminal works of American literature, and the writings of Shakespeare. The standards appropriately defer the many remaining decisions about what and how to teach to states, districts, and schools.[84]

Conclusion

It is precisely the Common Core State Curriculum, as stated before, that the 2016 Republican platform rejected with U.S. Secretary of Education Betsy DeVos, favoring an unregulated free market of schools using vouchers. Ironically, given the past history of Republican concerns, this approach could allow for the operation of charter schools reflecting a variety of cultures and languages.

Notes

1 Drew Westen, *The Political Brain: The Role of Emotion in Deciding the Fate of the Nation* (New York: Public Affairs, 2007), pp. 145–169.
2 "Republican platform 2016," p. i. Retrieved from https://gop.com/platform/ on November 23, 2016.
3 For the 1962 school prayer decision see, United States Courts, "Facts and Case Summary—Engel v. Vitale." Retrieved from www.uscourts.gov/educational-resources/educational-activities/facts-and-case-summary-engel-v-vitale on December 19, 2016.
4 For the 1963 Bible decision see, OYEZ IIT Chicago-Kent College of Law, "Abington School District v. Schempp." Retrieved from www.oyez.org/cases/1962/142 on December 19, 2016.
5 See OYEZ IIT Chicago-Kent College of Law, "Roe v. Wade." Retrieved from www.oyez.org/cases/1971/70-18 on December 19, 2016.
6 See Joel Spring, *American School, the American School: 1642–1993* (New York: McGraw-Hill, 1994), pp. 406–414.
7 Ralph Reed, *Active Faith: How Christians Are Changing the Soul of American Politics* (New York: Free Press, 1996), p. 105.
8 Ibid., p. 9.
9 Quoted in Jacob Weisberg, "Fear and Self-Loathing," *New York Times*, August 19, 1996, p. 36.
10 Ibid., p. 36.
11 Reed, *Active Faith*, pp. 4, 11.
12 Patrick J. Buchanan, *Right from the Beginning* (Washington, DC: Regnery Gateway, 1990), p. 6.
13 Reed, *Active Faith*, pp. 109–111.
14 Ibid., p. 111.

15 The American Presidency Project, "Republican Party platform of 1996," August 12, 1996, p. 33. Retrieved from www.presidency.ucsb.edu/ws/?pid=25848 on December 20, 2016.

16 "Republican platform 2016," p. 12. Retrieved from https://gop.com/platform/ on November 23, 2016.

17 Christian Coalition, "About Us." Retrieved from www.cc.org/about_us on December 20, 2016.

18 Ibid.

19 "About Us." Retrieved from www.cc.org/about_us on March 5, 2004.

20 Christian Coalition, "Take Action." Retrieved from www.cc.org/take_action on December 20, 2016.

21 Christian Coalition, "Voter Guides." Retrieved from www.cc.org/webform/2016_voter_guide_project on December 20, 2016.

22 "Dos and Don'ts." Retrieved from www.cc.org on March 2, 2005.

23 Ibid.

24 Ibid.

25 Public Law 107-110, 107th Congress, January 8, 2002 [H.R. 1], "No Child Left Behind Act of 2001" (Washington, DC: U.S. Government Printing Office, 2002).

26 U.S. Department of Education, "No Child Left Behind and Faith-Based Leaders: Working Together So All Children Succeed," U.S. Department of Education (Washington, DC: U.S. Government Printing Office, 2004). Retrieved from www.ed.gov/nclb/freedom/faith/leaders.pdf on January 7, 2005.

27 Ibid.

28 Roderick Paige, "White House Conference on Faith-Based and Community Initiatives," U.S. Department of Education. Retrieved from www.ed.gov/news/speeches/2002/10/10102002.html on March 7, 2004.

29 Press Release, "Paige Names John Porter as Director of Department's Center for Faith-Based and Community Initiatives," U.S. Department of Education, May 29, 2002. Retrieved from www.ed.gov/news/pressreleases/2002/05/05292002a.html on April 10, 2003.

30 Press Release, "Character Education Grants Awarded," U.S. Department of Education, September 29, 2003. Retrieved from www.ed.gov/news/pressreleases/2003/09/09292003.html on December 10, 2003.

31 Public Law 107-110, January 8, 2002, "No Child Left Behind Act of 2001," U.S. Department of Education, pp. 240–241. Retrieved from www.ed.gov/policy/elsec/leg/esea02/107-110.pdf on April 2, 2009.

32 Ibid., p. 393.

33 Ibid., pp. 394–395.

34 Press Release, "Character Education Grants Awarded. . . ."

35 Debra Viadero, "Proof of Positive Effect Found for Only a Few Character Programs," June 20, 2007. Retrieved from www.edweek.org on April 3, 2009.

36 "No Child Left Behind Act of 2001 . . . ," pp. 556–557.

37 Joan Delfattore, *What Johnny Shouldn't Read: Textbook Censorship in America* (New Haven, CT: Yale University Press, 1992), p. 14.

38 Ibid., pp. 36–60.

39 Ibid., pp. 61–75.

40 Ibid., pp. 76–79.

41 Ibid., p. 81.

42 Ibid., p. 87.

43 Reed, *Active Faith* . . ., pp. 117–118.

44 Haley Barbour, *Agenda for America: A Republican Direction for the Future* (Washington, DC: Regnery, 1996), p. 159.

45 Reed, *Active Faith . . .*, p. 118.
46 See Eric Schmitt, "Church Leaders Split on Plan for School Prayer Amendment," *New York Times*, July 24, 1995, p. A16.
47 Ibid., p. A16.
48 Ibid.
49 U.S. Department of Education, "Guidance on Constitutionally Protected Prayer in Public Elementary and Secondary Schools," February 7, 2003. Retrieved from www.ed.gov/policy/gen/guid/religionandschools/prayer_guidance.html on March 7, 2003.
50 Ibid.
51 "Republican platform of 2008. . . ," pp. 44–45.
52 The American Presidency Project, "We Believe in America: 2012 Republican platform," p. 12. Retrieved from www.presidency.ucsb.edu/ws/?pid=101961 on December 20, 2016.
53 "Republican platform 2016," p. 34. Retrieved from https://gop.com/platform/ on November 23, 2016.
54 William J. Bennett, *The De-Valuing of America: The Fight for Our Culture and Our Children* (New York: Simon & Schuster, 1992), p. 170.
55 Ibid., p. 170.
56 Ibid., p. 26.
57 Lynne Cheney, *American Memory* (Washington, DC: National Endowment for the Humanities, 1987).
58 Quoted in "Humanities Instruction Is Assailed," *Education Week*, September 9, 1987. Retrieved from www.edweek.org on March 2, 2008.
59 Ibid.
60 "Republican Party platform of 1996," American Presidency Project Document Archive, p. 48. Retrieved from www.presidency.ucsb.edu/ws/?pid=25848 on March 26, 2009.
61 Ibid., p. 37.
62 Quoted in Ibid.
63 Ibid.
64 "Republican Party platform of 2000," American Presidency Project Document Archive, p. 33. Retrieved from www.presidency.ucsb.edu/ws/?pid=25849 on March 26, 2009.
65 Ibid., p. 33.
66 Ibid.
67 "Diane Ravitch Curriculum Vitae." Retrieved from www.dianeravitch.com/vita.html on March 28, 2009.
68 Catherine Cornbleth and Dexter Waugh, *The Great Speckled Bird: Multicultural Politics and Education Policymaking* (Mahwah, NJ: Lawrence Erlbaum Associates, Inc., 1995), pp. 16–17, 68–71.
69 Ibid., 93–185.
70 Arthur M. Schlesinger, Jr., *The Disuniting of America* (Knoxville, TN: Whittle Direct Books, 1991), p. 8.
71 Quoted in Cornbleth and Waugh, *The Great Speckled Bird*, p. 85.
72 Quoted Ibid., p. 65.
73 Quoted in Ibid.
74 Quoted in Ibid.
75 Bob Dole and Jack Kemp, *Trusting the People: The Dole-Kemp Plan to Free the Economy and Create a Better America* (New York: Harper Collins, 1996), p. 92.
76 Dinesh D'Souza, *Illiberal Education: The Politics of Race and Sex on Campus* (New York: Vintage Books, 1992), and *The End of Racism* (New York: Free Press, 1995).
77 Ibid., p. 42.
78 "Republican platform 2016," p. 33. Retrieved from https://gop.com/platform/ on November 23, 2016.
79 Ibid.

80 Public Law 107-110, 107th Congress, January 8, 2002 [H.R. 1], "No Child Left Behind Act of 2001, Title III—Language Instruction for Limited English Proficient and Immigrant Students" (Washington, DC: U.S. Government Printing Office, 2002). For a political history of No Child Left Behind, see Patrick J. McGuin, *No Child Left Behind and the Transformation of Federal Education Policy, 1965–2005* (Lawrence, KS: University of Kansas Press, 2006).

81 Ibid.

82 Common Core State Standards, "Frequently Asked Questions." Retrieved from www. corestandards.org/ on January 6, 2013.

83 Common Core State Standards, "About the Standards." Retrieved from www.core standards.org/about-the-standards on January 5, 2013.

84 Ibid.

3

DEMOCRATS

Provide Quality and Affordable Public Education

Since the 1960s, the Democratic education agenda has stressed human capital economics, which asserts that investment in public education will reduce poverty and grow the economy. As I discuss later in this chapter, there are problems with human capital theory, particularly the idea that education is a solution for poverty and income inequalities. Can investment in education grow the economy and end poverty, or does it require other approaches?[1]

Human capital theory and civil rights concerns are reflected in the Democratic pursuit of equal education opportunity, including racial and economic school segregation and ensuring equal funding of all public schools. However, as admitted in the 2016 Democratic platform, equality of educational opportunity has not been achieved since the 1960s: "Our schools are more segregated today than they were when *Brown v. Board of Education* was decided, and we see wide disparities in educational outcomes across racial and socioeconomic lines . . . Democrats know that every child, no matter who they are, how much their families earn, or where they live, should have access to a high-quality education, from preschool through high school and beyond."[2]

In contrast to the 2016 Republican platform's stress on free markets supported by religious values, the 2016 Democratic platform asserts: "Out of many, we are one. . . . Democrats believe that cooperation is better than conflict, unity is better than division, empowerment is better than resentment, and bridges are better than walls."[3]

Also, in opposition to the 2016 Republican call for school choice to enhance free market competition between schools, including for-profit schools, the 2016 Democratic platform continues support of public schools: "We support democratically governed, great neighborhood public schools and high-quality public charter schools, and we will help them disseminate best practices to other school leaders and educators."[4]

The 2016 Democratic platform specifically rejects Republican support of for-profit schools: "Democrats oppose for-profit charter schools focused on making a profit off of public resources. We believe that high-quality public charter schools should provide options for parents, but should not replace or destabilize traditional public schools."[5] Worried that charter schools are contributing to inequality of education opportunity, the platform insists: "Charter schools must reflect their communities, and thus must accept and retain proportionate numbers of students of color, students with disabilities and English Language Learners in relation to their neighborhood public schools. We support increased transparency and accountability for all charter schools."[6]

Issues in the Democratic Agenda

As I will discuss, investment in education (human capital theory) has not ended poverty, reduced income inequalities or increased the number of available jobs. Also, despite a focus on equal educational opportunity since the 1960s, why, as admitted in the 2016 platform, has racial and economic segregation of schools increased? Is there a flaw in Democratic educational proposals? I will first examine problems in human capital theory.

Democrats have claimed a close connection between education, poverty and economic growth. One question about this connection is whether low-quality schooling causes poverty and income inequalities, or are these primarily caused by other factors, such as the availability of jobs, the tax structure or decisions made by corporations? Is improved education the key to global economic competition or is it other factors, such as the movement of companies and jobs to other countries or the failure to invest in the infrastructure? In addition, there are no longitudinal research studies demonstrating that educational investments improve the economy, reduce poverty and income inequalities and make the U.S. more competitive in the global economic system.

Human Capital: Education, Poverty and the Elementary and Secondary Education Act

Since the 1960's War on Poverty, the Democratic Party has pursued federal policies to end inequality of educational opportunity and equality of economic opportunity. The War on Poverty was launched during Democratic President Lyndon Johnson's administration (November 22, 1963–January 20, 1969). The most important education legislation of the period was Title I of the 1965 Elementary and Secondary Education Act (ESEA), which in 2001 became No Child Left Behind. Since the 1990s Democrats claimed improving the school system was key to improving America's economic system in global markets. In 1992, Democratic President Bill Clinton ran on a platform that declared: "A competitive American economy requires the global market's best educated, best trained, most flexible work force."[7]

Title I of ESEA, signed by President Johnson on April 11, 1965, provided funds for improved educational programs for children designated as "educationally deprived." The original Title I, "declares it to be the policy of the United States to provide financial assistance . . . to expand and improve . . . educational programs by various means . . . which contribute particularly to meeting the special educational needs of educationally deprived children." Rather than "deprived children," 2001 No Child Left Behind uses the term "disadvantaged" and opens, "TITLE I—IMPROVING THE ACADEMIC ACHIEVEMENT OF THE DISADVANTAGED."[8]

Title I, along with the preschool program Head Start, were the major educational components of the War on Poverty. At the opening of congressional hearings on ESEA, Secretary of Health, Education, and Welfare Anthony J. Celebrezze provided a justification and rationale for special educational assistance to the "educationally deprived." Celebrezze claimed, "The President's program . . . is designed to break this cycle [of poverty] which has been running on from generation to generation in this most affluent period of our history." He stated that a clear link exists between high educational attainment and high economic attainment.[9]

Support for Secretary Celebrezze's argument was contained in a highly influential 1964 report by Walter Heller, chairman of the President's Council of Economic Advisors. A section in the Council's annual report titled "The Problem of Poverty in America," gave education a central role in combating poverty: "Equality of opportunity is the American dream, and universal education our noblest pledge to realize it. But, for the children of the poor, education is a handicap race; many are too ill motivated at home to learn at school."[10] Also, the report claimed, "The chief reason for low rates of pay is low productivity, which in turn can reflect lack of education or training, physical and mental disability, or poor motivation."[11]

The Heller report linked education and poverty: "The importance of education as a factor in poverty is suggested by the fact that families headed by persons with no more than 8 years of education have an incidence rate [poverty] of 37 percent."[12] Claiming that educating children from low-income families was the key to ending poverty, the report stressed the importance of preschool education: "This often means that schooling must start on a pre-school basis and include a broad range of more intensive services."[13]

A major source of the War on Poverty arguments that education, including preschool, could reduce poverty originated in the work of economists Theodore Shultz and Gary Becker.[14] In 1961, Theodore Shultz stated, "economists have long known that people are an important part of the wealth of nations."[15] He argued that people invested in education to improve their job opportunities. In a similar fashion, nations could invest to increase educational opportunities as a stimulus for economic growth. In his original 1964 book on human capital, Gary Becker asserted that economic growth now depended on the knowledge, information, ideas, skills and health of the workforce. Investments in education, he argued, could improve human capital, which would contribute to economic growth.[16] Later, he used the term *knowledge* economy: "An economy like that of the United States is called a capitalist economy, but the more accurate term is human capital or *knowledge* capital economy."[17] Becker claimed that human capital represented three-fourths of the wealth of the United States and that investment in education would be the key to further economic growth.

After the 1960s, the Democratic Party continued to campaign for preschool education as a means of achieving equality of educational opportunity. In the 1972 election, the Democratic Party took the bold step of advocating universal child care programs as part of its "Rights of Children." The platform declared: "We call for the federal government to fund comprehensive development child care programs that will be family centered, locally controlled and universally available."[18] The Democrats included early childhood education and health services in the proposal, calling for universal child care: "Health, social service and early childhood education should be part of these programs, as well as a variety of options most appropriate to their needs."[19]

When President Bill Clinton was elected in 1992, the Democratic Party maintained its support for Head Start and child care. The 2000 Democratic platform referred to new research showing that, "High-quality preschool should no longer be a luxury. Research . . . shows that giving kids a smart start can lead to higher reading and achievement levels, higher graduation rates, and greater success in the workplace."[20]

The emphasis on preschool as a poverty reduction program continued into President Obama's administration. In the Democratic 2008 platform's section "Poverty," it was stated, "Working together, *we can cut poverty in half within ten years*. We will provide all our children a world-class education, from *early childhood through college* [author's emphasis]."[21] In his 2013 State of the Union Address, Democratic President Obama stressed preschool education: "And for poor kids who need help the most, this lack of access to preschool education can shadow them for the rest of their lives. So, tonight, I propose working with states to make high-quality preschool available to every single child in America. Every dollar we invest in high-quality early childhood education can save more than seven dollars later on, by boosting graduation rates, reducing teen pregnancy, even reducing violent crime."[22]

Democrats for Education Reform: Continuing the War on Poverty

Continuing to advocate education as an economic cure-all, a group having major influence over President Obama's education policies, the Democrats for Education

Reform, broke with traditional Democratic political alliances by asserting that the teachers unions and the school establishment were a major source of educational inequalities. The group's "Statement of Principles" asserted, "These systems [public schools], once viewed romantically as avenues of opportunity for all, have become captive to powerful, entrenched interests that too often put the demands of adults before the educational needs of children. This perverse hierarchy of priorities is political, and thus requires a political response."[23]

Who were these "entrenched interests?" According to the Democrats for Education Reform, they were the teachers unions, local and state public school bureaucracies and teacher training institutions. These "entrenched interests," according to the group, were hindering the ability to:

1. Evaluate and fire poor teachers and to establish alternative pathways to teacher certification: "All states and districts should begin moving immediately to create teacher evaluation systems comprised of multiple measures that are part a single statewide assessment of teacher effectiveness";[24]
2. Provide greater parental school choice by expanding public charter schools: "We support mechanisms that allow parents to select excellent schools for their children, and where education dollars follow each child to their school";[25]
3. Create national curriculum standards: "We support clearly-articulated national standards and expectations for core subject areas, while allowing states and local districts to determine how best to make sure that all students are reaching those standards" and "We support policies which stimulate the creation of new, accountable public schools and which simultaneously close down failing schools."[26]

Like previous Democrats, Democrats for Education Reform wanted to reduce educational inequalities:

> A first-rate system of public education is the cornerstone of a prosperous, free and just society, yet millions of American children today—particularly low-income and children of color—are trapped in persistently failing schools that are part of deeply dysfunctional school systems.[27]

Charter Schools and Poverty

The Obama administration recommended expansion of public charter schools, in contrast to for-profit charter schools, to provide alternatives to low-income students.[28] In the past, charter schools were promoted as giving all parents more educational choices. In the Obama administration, charter schools were to meet the needs of "disadvantaged" students. In this context, charter schools became part of a new war on poverty. For instance, Lisa Macfarlane, Democrats for Education

Reform Washington State Director, defended charter schools in Washington State by emphasizing their service to "disadvantaged" students: "Our country's top Democrat, Barack Obama, the man we all fought to elect, is a big charter school fan. He believes in the ability of *successful charter schools to help some of our most educationally disadvantaged kids* [author's emphasis]."[29] She provided the following reasons for supporting charter schools:

- High-quality public charter schools are successfully closing achievement gaps.
- High-quality public charter schools can give underserved parents a choice and voice in their education.[30]

The Democrats for Education Reform's brief, "Public Charter Schools and High-Quality Pre-K," asserted that charter schools are a solution for educating children from low-income families. Both charter schools and Pre-K education were to be part of a new war on poverty. The brief asserts:

> Research shows that between one-third and one-half of the achievement gap already exists by the time children begin first grade. Children from low-income families receive less support for early language, literacy, cognitive and social-emotional development than their more affluent peers. By age three, the typical disadvantaged child has heard 30 million fewer words than children from affluent families. Low-income children are also less likely to be read to and watch more TV than their middle-class and affluent peers. Low-income families are often under increased economic and other stresses that can also negatively affect children's development.[31]

The brief proposed: "States should enact policies to encourage the creation of Pre-K Charter Schools to deliver high-quality early education to 3- and 4-year-olds. At a time when state budget woes threaten many Pre-K investments, this approach would enable states to use stimulus funds to expand children's access to high-quality early education programs, while maintaining a diverse, publicly accountable network of Pre-K providers."[32] Its recommendations included:

1. Ensuring that the state's charter school law explicitly authorizes charter schools to offer Pre-K programs;
2. Amending the state charter school law and/or the state school funding formula law to allow public charter schools that serve 3- and 4-year-olds to receive per pupil funds for these students through the state's school funding formula;
3. Exempting Pre-K charters from state caps on the number of charter schools that may be opened. This allows states to use Pre-K chartering to expand access to quality early education without bumping up against state charter school caps.[33]

The recommendations of Democrats for Education Reform that Pre-K education and charter schools be targeted for "disadvantaged" students (the terms used to describe this set of students vary, and in the Race to the Top, they are described as "high-need") were included in the Race to the Top:

> The Secretary is particularly interested in applications that include practices, strategies, or programs to improve educational outcomes for *high-need students* who are young children (pre-kindergarten through third grade) by enhancing the quality of preschool programs. Of particular interest are proposals that support practices that (i) improve school readiness (including social, emotional, and cognitive); and (ii) improve the transition between preschool and kindergarten [author's emphasis].[34]

President Obama's Race to the Top encouraged the development of charter schools by providing incentives for States to increase the number of charter schools. In the words of Race to the Top, a State's "charter school law ... [should] not prohibit or effectively inhibit increasing the number of high-performing charter schools."[35]

2016: Hillary Clinton and Preschool

The 2016 Democratic platform advocated universal preschool in the context of educating a global workforce. As discussed earlier in this chapter, there is no clear research that demonstrates a causality between preschool and an improved workforce. The 2016 platform states: "Democrats believe we must have the best-educated population and workforce in the world. That means making early childhood education and universal preschool a priority, especially in light of new research showing how much early learning can impact life-long success."[36] The 2016 platform continued support of the 1960's War on Poverty Head Start program: "Democrats will invest in early childhood programs like Early Head Start and provide every family in America with access to high-quality child care and high-quality preschool programs."[37]

Similar to the 1960s War on Poverty, 2016 Democratic support of preschool was embedded in recognition of other conditions causing poverty. The 2016 platform declares:

> The Democratic Party is committed to eliminating opportunity gaps—particularly those that lead to students from low-income communities arriving on day one of kindergarten several years behind their peers. This means advocating for labor and public assistance laws that ensure poor parents can spend time with their children. This means raising household incomes in poor communities. It means ensuring children have health care, stable housing free of contaminants, and a community free of violence in order to minimize the likelihood of cognitive delays.[38]

Preschool, as part of a solution for poverty, became part of Hillary Clinton's 2016 presidential campaign. She stressed universal preschool as preparation for low-income students to enter the labor force. Clinton asserted: "I believe getting off to a good start should be our children's birthright, part of the basic bargain that we have with each other as a nation. Every child should have the tools and the skills to thrive in tomorrow's economy, especially those kids from our most vulnerable and at-risk communities."[39]

On her presidential campaign website, Hillary Clinton continued to emphasize support for preschool for low-income students and those with limited English abilities:

> Expanding early childhood education has been close to Hillary Clinton's heart throughout her career. As first lady of Arkansas, she introduced the Home Instruction for Parents of Preschool Youngsters (HIPPY) program, which helps parents teach their children at home before they begin kindergarten. As a U.S. senator, she called for a national initiative to help establish high-quality pre-K programs, including providing pre-K at no cost to children from low-income homes and homes with limited English speaking.[40]

Candidate Clinton also included concerns about child care and child care workers. Republicans might complain that these proposals could undermine the role of parents in raising their children by calling for support of the child care industry. Should financial aid or the tax structure ensure that at least one parent be able to raise his/her child rather than turning it over to preschool and child care workers? Hillary Clinton's campaign website stated:

As president, Hillary will:

- Make preschool universal for every 4-year-old in America.
- Improve the quality of child care and early learning by giving a RAISE to America's child care workforce.
- Significantly increase child care investments so that no family in America has to pay more than 10 percent of its income to afford high-quality child care.
- Double our investment in Early Head Start and the Early Head Start-Child Care Partnership program.
- Award scholarships of up to $1,500 per year to help as many as 1 million student parents afford high-quality child care.
- Increase access to high-quality child care on college campuses by serving an additional 250,000 children.[41]

In summary, Democratic preschool and child care proposals are primarily focused on the economy. However, we have no proof that preschool will boost economic growth and improve the workforce. While one might applaud support of child care services and workers, it can often imply that both parents are expected to enter the workforce rather than one parent staying home to provide child care. Of course, single-parent families required to work would benefit from expanded preschool and improved child care services. In two-parent families, should we focus on policies that allow at least one parent to stay home for childrearing?

Is the emphasis on preschool and child care leading to what Bruce Fuller calls *Standardized Childhood*,[42] where one theory of an ideal childrearing method comes to dominate preschools and child care services? Of course, many might argue that a standardized childhood might not be possible given all the religious and cultural differences about how children should be raised.

Common Curriculum Standards to End Inequality of Educational Opportunity

Until the 2016 election, many Democrats and Republicans supported national and state curriculum standards to ensure that all students were exposed to the same academic content. This was in reaction to claims that students attending schools serving low-income families were not being taught the same quality curriculum as students attending schools serving middle-income families. Breaking with past support for state or federal curriculum standards, the 2016 Democratic platform simply stated: "Democrats believe all students should be taught to high academic standards. Schools should have adequate resources to provide programs and support to help meet the needs of every child."[43]

This simple support for "high academic standards" was in contrast to Democratic and Republican support of the 2001 federal legislation No Child Left Behind, which required States to create academic standards for all public schools. In 2010, the National Governor Association released Common Core State Standards with the expectation that they would be adopted by all states.

Combined with the Democratic platform's vague support of high academic standards, the 2016 election seemed to doom efforts at a national set of curriculum standards to reduce educational inequalities. The 2016 Republican platform rejected Common Core State Standards: "We likewise repeat our longstanding opposition to the imposition of national standards and assessments, encourage the parents and educators who are implementing alternatives to Common Core, and congratulate the states which have successfully repealed it."[44]

Jonathan Kozol's 1991 *Savage Inequalities: Children in America's Schools*[45] fueled early concern about inequality of educational opportunity in curricula. Kozol painted a bleak picture of the differences between rich and poor public schools. Ensconced in protected suburbs, the rich and almost rich, according to Kozol, could provide their children with public schools filled with small classes, up-to-date educational materials, the best teachers and an easy path to college. In contrast, the poor, often represented in the book as racial minorities, attended schools with deteriorating buildings, classes with too many students, outdated educational materials and poor teachers. Writing in *Time* magazine, Emily Mitchell commented, "Kozol has written a searing exposé of the extremes of wealth and poverty in America's school system and the blighting effect on poor children."[46]

Kozol's book sparked concerns about the curriculum taught to low-income students and their classroom environment. While only referring to "high standards," in the 2016 Democratic platform, the document does reflect concern about equality of instructional conditions: "Schools should have adequate resources to provide programs and support to help meet the needs of every child. We will hold schools, districts, communities, and states accountable for raising achievement levels for all students—particularly low-income students, students of color, English Language Learners, and students with disabilities."[47]

Reflecting concerns raised by Kozol, for instance, standards and accountability were part of the legislation signed by Democratic President Bill Clinton in 1994 called the Goals 2000: Educate America Act. Unlike the later No Child Left Behind legislation, the academic standards proposed in this legislation were to be voluntary. In supporting the Goals 2000: Educate America Act, Democrats accepted the unproven assumption that increasing educational standards and making schools accountable would support equality of educational opportunity and, in the framework of human capital arguments, improve the schooling of the American workforce and consequently increase worker wages and decrease economic inequalities. Two months after the signing of the legislation, Marshall Smith, Clinton's undersecretary of education, speaking at a Brookings Institute conference on national standards asserted: "The need for American students to learn more demanding content and skills became increasingly clear in the 1980s. The United States faces great challenges: internally, by the need to maintain a strong democracy in a complex and diverse society; externally, by a competitive economic environment that will be dominated by high-skills jobs."[48] Marshall repeated an unquestioned assumption of the standards movement that children will learn more if they are challenged by more difficult standards. Concerning Clinton's Goals 2000 legislation, Marshall contended that high academic standards will result in high academic achievement for all students because "it builds on our understanding that all children can learn to higher levels than we have previously thought."[49]

Democratic strategy assumed that under the new standards all students would have equal access to the teachers, books, educational materials and laboratories required to meet national or state academic standards. Goals 2000: Educate America Act and Improving America's Schools Act represented an important change in the Democrats' traditional concern with equality of educational opportunity. The emphasis was no longer on desegregation and compensatory education programs. Now the focus was on uniformity through application of the same standards and accountability to all U.S. children. In this context, equality of educational opportunity meant equality of curricula, or in other words, every student would have an equal chance to learn a uniform state curriculum.

The Goals 2000: Educate America Act was also to overcome "savage inequalities" in the American school system. The legislation introduced opportunity-to-learn (OTL) standards as "the criteria for . . . assessing . . . [the ability] of the education system . . . to provide all students with an opportunity to learn the material in voluntary national content standards or state content standards."[50] This meant that educational and other experts would have to find "scientific" measurements of school inequalities. The OTL standards held out the hope of finally addressing the issue of inequalities in educational opportunity. In the past, Republicans and Democrats skillfully avoided the politically charged issue of equal funding of school systems. Upper- and middle-class suburbanites were unwilling to give up their educational advantages, and they resisted being taxed to upgrade poorer school districts.[51]

Discussion of OTL standards disappeared in debates testing resulting form No Child Left Behind and the Common Core State Standards. According to Andrew Porter of the Wisconsin Center for Education Research, one of the federal government's experts hired to make scientific sense of the standards: "The initial motivation for OTL standards stems from an equity concern that high-stakes assessments of student achievement are fair only if students have had an adequate opportunity to learn the content assessed in those high-stakes tests."[52] Can there be equal preparation for high-stakes tests if some students attend overcrowded and deteriorating classrooms and they do not have access to high-quality academic courses? How can students be adequately prepared for testing if their teachers are not prepared and do not have professional environments in which to work? The following is a list of some OTL recommendations targeting learning environments, curricula and quality teachers that would give students an equal opportunity for high scores on tests required by No Child Left Behind:

- Schools should have enough physical space to accommodate all their students safely.
- Schools should have an adequate number of teachers and classrooms to ensure optimum class size.
- Students should have access to textbooks and educational facilities.
- Teachers should have the materials, time, private space and support staff they need for lesson preparation and professional development.
- All students should have access to high level courses that will allow them to meet performance and content standards and provide them with good career opportunities.[53]

The OTL standards did not gain support in the 1994 Congress and disappeared from later standards discussion. Increased funding of Head Start and preschool programs Democrats claimed would prepare all students for academic standards and high-stakes testing. Support for preschool as an answer for inequality of educational opportunity persisted through to the 2016 Democratic platform, which claims: "the United States still lags behind other advanced economies in providing high-quality, universal preschool programs to help all of our kids get a *strong start to their educations* [author's emphasis].[54]

In President Bill Clinton's last inaugural address, he limited his educational comments to educational standards and the knowledge required by the global economy. There was no mention of OTL standards that would ensure equality of educational opportunity in meeting the standards outlined in Goals 2000. Clinton said,

> Our schools will have the highest standards in the world, igniting the spark of possibility in the eyes of every girl and every boy. And the doors of higher education will be open to all. The knowledge and power of the information age will be within reach not just of the few but of every classroom, every library, every child. Parents and children will have time not only to work but to read and play together. And the plans they make at their kitchen table will be those of a better home, a better job, the certain chance to go to college.[55]

After the 2000 election of President George W. Bush, Democrats were quick to accuse President Bush of stealing their ideas after passage in 2001 of No Child Left Behind. The accusation was based on President Clinton's championship of standards and accountability and Democratic candidate Al Gore's reiteration of the Democratic vision of the standards movement during his failed 2000 Democratic campaign. During the 2000 campaign Gore published an education agenda containing what was becoming a familiar theme based on human capital arguments that school standards were necessary for global competition. The Gore agenda asserted that he would "build on and extend the aggressive efforts since 1993 to improve our schools through higher standards, extra help to students who need it the most, and equal access to higher education."[56] In other words, No Child Left Behind was to ensure equality of educational opportunity by teaching a standardized curriculum to all students and holding all schools accountable through standardized testing of all students.

The 2004 Democratic presidential candidate John Kerry supported No Child Left Behind. In the Democratic campaign book, *Our Plan for America: Stronger At Home, Respected in the World*, Kerry highlighted that he voted for the legislation.[57] So by the 2008 election, Democrats were committed to some form of national or state academic standards and high-stakes testing.

Democratic President Barack Obama supported national curriculum standards. Democrats for Education Reform proposed to President Obama "World Class Standards and Assessments," which called for a "seamless, integrated state system of P-16 education."[58] The Democrats for Education Reform linked common standards directly to the needs of the global economy: "It is widely agreed that the

U.S. should: raise academic standards, in-line with global economic demands for a college-educated, high-tech workforce."[59] The Obama administration was warned to avoid past errors in trying to create national curriculum standards, including ensuring companies producing tests aligned them with national standards: "This time around, the federal government must ensure that states and the major testing companies break the patterns that have rendered mediocre and unimaginative assessment products in the past."[60] This issue will be discussed in Chapter 4 when I consider the profits gained by companies with the implementation of Common Core State Standards, particularly the testing and textbook giant Pearson.

The Race to the Top rejected the idea of P-16 standards and limited them to P-12. President Obama's Race to the Top called for: "Adopting standards and assessments that prepare students to succeed in college and the workplace and to compete in the global economy."[61]

Preparing students for the global economy was the major goal of the Common Core State Standards released by the National Governors Association in 2010. As officially stated, the Common Core State Standards were to prepare students to enter a global workforce:

> The Common Core State Standards provide a consistent, clear understanding of what students are expected to learn, so teachers and parents know what they need to do to help them. The standards are designed to be robust and relevant to the real world, *reflecting the knowledge and skills that our young people need for success in college and careers. With American students fully prepared for the future, our communities will be best positioned to compete successfully in the global economy* [author's emphasis].[62]

In summary, what happened to attempts to ensure equality of educational opportunity by exposing all students, rich and poor, to the same academic standards? After many years of debate over the issue the idea of national standards they seem to have tossed into the dustbin of history. Discussions of national curriculum standards disappeared from the 2016 Democratic agenda. Between the 1990s and 2016, Democrats were committed to supporting academic standards to provide equality of educational opportunities and to enhance America's ability to compete in the global economy. Along the way, Democrats abandoned OTL standards in favor of closing and/or restructuring failing schools to achieve equality of educational opportunity. Avoiding the political debate over national standards, the 2016 Democratic platform, as discussed previously, just called for high standards.

Democrats and the Testing Controversy: Opt Out and FairTest

Unexpectedly there was a strong backlash to the standardized testing required by No Child Left Behind and many state governments. As a result, there was an Opt

Out movement by parents to keep students home on standardized testing days. FairTest: The National Center for Fair and Open Testing played an important role in this movement. The organization posted the following:

> Testing overuse and misuse is damaging public education by eating up classroom time, narrowing curriculum and driving many students out of school. It is perpetuating a false narrative of failure and putting schools in low-income communities at risk of closure or privatization.
>
> "Opting out," or refusing to take government-mandated standardized tests, is a powerful way to protest this educational malpractice. Nationally, hundreds of thousands of parents, teachers and students are fighting back against high-stakes testing overkill by exercising their right to opt out, boycott or refuse. It's one way to educate others about how the harms of excessive testing and an important way to tell policymakers they must change course.
>
> The exploding opt-out movement has already achieved its first victories. It is altering state and local testing policies for the better, reducing the number of tests and lowering their stakes. A larger, stronger out-out movement will win even more substantial assessment reforms.[63]

This protest movement resulted in Democrats including the surprising statement in their 2016 platform: "We support enabling parents to opt their children out of standardized tests without penalty for either the student or their school."[64]

In certainly one of the first national platforms to worry too much testing, the Democrats in 2016 devoted a long section to the issue that doomed the argument that standardized testing would be a vehicle for achieving equality of educational opportunity:

> We are also deeply committed to ensuring that we strike a better balance on testing so that it informs, but does not drive, instruction. To that end, we encourage states to develop a multiple measures approach to assessment, and we believe that standardized tests must be reliable and valid. We oppose high-stakes standardized tests that falsely and unfairly label students of color, students with disabilities and English Language Learners as failing; the use of standardized test scores as basis for refusing to fund schools or to close schools.[65]

Democrats and Quality Teachers

A discussion of differences in teachers serving low-income students and those working in districts serving affluent students was one result of the previously mentioned Jonathan Kozol's *Death at an Early Age*. How could you achieve equality of educational opportunity with inequalities between districts in the quality of their teaching staffs? Were there training and evaluation methods that would ensure that all students had quality teachers?

A highly controversial approach to the issue was the use of student tests scores to evaluate teachers. The 2016 Democratic platform specifically rejected "the use of student test scores in teacher and principal evaluations, a practice which has been repeatedly rejected by researchers." The platform asserted: "We know that good teachers are essential to improving student learning and helping all students to meet high academic standards. Democrats will launch a national campaign to recruit and retain high-quality teachers. We will ensure that teachers receive the tools and ongoing professional development they need to succeed in the classroom and provide our children with a world-class education."[66] It was not specified how high-quality teachers could be recruited or what were the best methods for teacher training.

Hillary Clinton's campaign promised to: "Launch a national campaign to modernize and elevate the profession of teaching."[67] Like many Democratic education proposals, Clinton's call for quality teachers was embedded in an economic argument: "America is asking more of our educators than ever before. They are preparing our kids *for a competitive economy* [author's emphasis]."[68] And, of course, providing quality teachers would contribute to equality of educational opportunity: "[teachers are] filling gaps that we as a country have neglected—like giving low-income kids, English-language learners, and kids with disabilities the support they need to thrive."[69]

Again, without any specificity of how this would occur, Clinton's campaign website proclaimed: "That's why Hillary will launch a national campaign to elevate and modernize the teaching profession, by preparing, supporting, and paying every child's teacher as if the future of our country is in their hands—because it is." Since most teacher salaries are determined by local school districts, this goal could only be achieved through federal support.

Conclusion

Human capital and free market theories characterize the differences between 2016 Democratic and Republican education agendas. Since the 1960s, Democrats have offered education proposals based on an unproven human capital theory that investment in education will solve the problem of poverty, grow the economy and end income inequality. Since the 1960s' Head Start program, Democrats have championed preschool as one of the solutions for poverty—again unproven. Currently, expansion of public charter schools, not for-profit charter schools, are also to contribute to poverty reduction.

The 2016 Democratic education agenda broke sharply with the party's previous efforts to achieve equality of educational opportunity. In 2016, standardized testing was criticized, which in the past was considered a means of judging whether or not schools were providing equality of educational opportunity. Also, in 2016, Democrats abandoned support of state and national academic standards that would ensure that children from low-income and high-income would be exposed to the same curriculum—the 2016 Democratic platform simply called for high standards. Also, by 2016, Democrats abandoned their call for Opportunity to Learn Standards to ensure equal quality schools for poor and rich students.

The 2016 Democratic platform offered no solutions for what was admitted to be increased segregation of schools: "Our schools are more segregated today than they were when *Brown v. Board of Education* was decided, and we see wide disparities in educational outcomes across racial and socioeconomic lines." There is evidence supporting the platform claim of more segregated schools resulting from No Child Left Behind and Race to the Top, both of which protected school districts and schools serving upper-income students from students from low-income family. Writing in the *New York Times* on May 19, 2012, David Kirp, professor of public policy at the University of California, Berkeley, argued,

> The failure of the No Child Left Behind regimen to narrow the achievement gap offers the sobering lesson that closing underperforming public schools, setting high expectations for students, getting tough with teachers and opening a raft of charter schools isn't the answer. If we're serious about improving educational opportunities, we need to revisit the abandoned policy of school integration.[70]

Economic and racial segregation have increased as reported in 2012 by the UCLA Civil Rights Project.[71] With the descriptive title "E Pluribus . . . Deepening Double Segregation for More Students," the report concludes:

> Segregation has increased dramatically across the country for Latino students, who are attending more intensely segregated and impoverished schools than they have for generations. . . . In spite of declining residential segregation for black families and large-scale movement to the suburbs in most parts of the country, school segregation remains very high for black students. It is also double segregation by both race and poverty.[72]

Racial and economic segregation for Latino students has increased since the 2001 No Child Left Behind legislation: "In the early 2000s, the average Latino and black student attended a school where a *little over half of the students* were low income (as measured by free and reduced price lunch eligibility), but now attend schools where low income students account for *nearly two-thirds of their classmates*."[73]

From the standpoint of the UCLA Civil Rights Project, Race to the Top passively allowed increased segregation resulting in "severely limit[ing] educational opportunities for African American and Latino students, as well as the opportunity for all students to learn to live and work effectively in a multiracial society."[74]

The UCLA Civil Rights project lends support to the argument that an implicit reason for supporting for NCLB and Race to the Top was to protect the educational privileges of public schools and school districts serving upper-income families. This might be considered an unwarranted suggestion since so much of the rhetoric surrounding these two pieces of legislation claims they will enhance educational opportunities for children from low-income families. The report states: "More recently . . . the Bush and Obama Administrations have vigorously fostered policies that reflected their passive attitude toward resegregation issues."[75]

As I discuss in the next chapter, the Race to the Top spurred the growth of the for-profit education industry. Also, in the next chapter, I will consider the 2016 Democratic concern with college student loans.

Notes

1 See Joel Spring, *Economization of Education: Human Capital Global Corporations, Skills-Based Schooling* (New York: Routledge, 2015).
2 "2016 Democratic Party platform," July 21, 2016, pp. 1. Retrieved from www.presidency.ucsb.edu/papers_pdf/117717.pdf January 10, 2017, p. 30.
3 Ibid., p. 1.
4 Ibid., p. 34.
5 Ibid.
6 Ibid.
7 Democratic Party platform of 1992, "A New Covenant with the American People," American Presidency Project Document Archive, July 13, 1992, p. 5. Retrieved from www.presidency.ucsb.edu/ws/index. php?pid=pid29610 on January 5, 2009.
8 Public Law 107-110, 107th Congress, January 8, 2002 [H.R. 1], "No Child Left Behind Act of 2001" (Washington, DC: U.S. Government Printing Office, 2002).
9 U.S. Congress, House Committee on Education and Labor, Aid to Elementary and Secondary Education: Hearings before the General Subcommittee on Education of the Committee on Education and Labor, 89th Cong., 1st sess., 1965 (Washington, DC: U.S. Government Printing Office, 1965), pp. 63–82.
10 "The Problem of Poverty in America," *The Annual Report of the Council of Economic Advisers* (Washington, DC: U.S. Government Printing Office, 1964).
11 Ibid.
12 Ibid.
13 Ibid.
14 See Brian Keeley, *Human Capital: How What You Know Shapes Your Life* (Paris: OECD, 2007), pp. 28–35; and Phillip Brown and Hugh Lauder, "Globalization, Knowledge and the Myth of the Magnet Economy," in *Education, Globalization and Social Change*, edited by Hugh Lauder, Phillip Brown, Jo-Anne Dillabough, and A. H. Halsey (Oxford: Oxford University Press, 2006), pp. 317–340.
15 Quoted in Keeley, *Human Capital*, p. 29.
16 Gary Becker, *Human Capital* (New York: Columbia University Press, 1964).
17 Gary Becker, "The Age of Human Capital," in *Education, Globalization and Social Change*, edited by Hugh Lauder, Phillip Brown, Jo-Anne Dillabough, and A. H. Halsey (Oxford: Oxford University Press, 2006), p. 292.
18 Democratic Party platform of 1972, "New Directions," American Presidency Project Document Archive, July 10, 1972, p. 19. Retrieved from www.presidency.ucsb.edu/ws/index.php?pid=29605 on January 14, 2009.
19 Ibid.

20 Democratic Party platform of 2000, "Prosperity, Progress, and Peace," American Presidency Project Document Archive, p. 9. Retrieved from www.presidency.ucsb. edu/ws/index.php?pid=29612 on January 5, 2009.

21 2008 Democratic Party platform, "Renewing America's Promise." Retrieved from www.presidency.ucsb.edu/ws/index.php?pid=78283 on February 22, 2013.

22 Barack Obama, "2013 State of the Union Address." Retrieved from www.whitehouse. gov/state-of-the-union-2013#webform on February 21, 2013.

23 Democrats for Education Reform, "Statement of Principles." Retrieved from www. dfer.org/petition/SOP/ on February 20, 2013.

24 Democrats for Education Reform, "Statement of Principles on Teacher Quality and Effectiveness in the Reauthorization of the Elementary and Secondary Education Act," October 7, 2011. Retrieved from www.dfer.org/ESEA%20Priorities%20Teacher%20 Quality.Coalition%20Letter.Final.pdf on February 20, 2013.

25 Democrats for Education Reform, "What We Stand For." Retrieved from www.dfer. org/about/standfor/ on February 20, 2013.

26 Ibid.

27 Democrats for Education Reform, "Statement of Principles. . . ."

28 Democrats for Education Reform, "Racing to the Top: American Recovery and Reinvestment Act Issues Brief Series#1: Public Charter Schools and High-Quality Pre-K." June 17, 2009. Retrieved from www.ucdenver.edu/academics/colleges/SPA/ researchandoutreach/Buechner%20Institute%20for%20Governance/Centers/CEPA/ EdStimulusFunds/Documents/Race_to_the_Top_1.pdf on February 21, 2013.

29 Lisa Macfarlane, "Why Democrats Support Charter Schools." Retrieved from www. dfer.org/2012/01/why_democrats_s.php on February 21, 2013.

30 Ibid.

31 Democrats for Education Reform, "Racing to the Top: American Recovery and Reinvestment Act Issues Brief Series#1: Public Charter Schools and High-Quality Pre-K. . . ," p. 4.

32 Ibid.

33 Ibid., pp. 6–7.

34 U.S. Department of Education, "Race to the Top Program: Executive Summary," November 2009, p. 4. Retrieved from http://www2.ed.gov/programs/racetothetop/ executive-summary.pdf on January 23, 2013.

35 Ibid., p. 11.

36 "2016 Democratic Party platform," p. 32.

37 Ibid., p. 32.

38 Ibid., p. 33.

39 Hillary Clinton, "Early Childhood Education," June 15, 2015. Retrieved from www. hillaryclinton.com/issues/early-childhood-education/ on January 15, 2017.

40 Ibid.

41 Ibid.

42 Bruce Fuller, *Standardized Childhood: The Political and Cultural Struggle Early Education* (Palo Alto, CA: Stanford University Press, 2007).

43 "2016 Democratic Party platform," p. 32.

44 "Republican platform 2016," p. 33. Retrieved from https://gop.com/platform/ on November 23, 2016.

45 Jonathan Kozol, *Savage Inequalities: Children in America's Schools* (New York: Crown, 1991).

46 Back cover of Ibid.

47 "2016 Democratic Party platform," p. 32.

48 Marshall S. Smith, "Education Reform in America's Public Schools: The Clinton Agenda," in *Debating the Future of American Education: Do We Need National Standards and Assessments?* edited by Diane Ravitch (Washington, DC: Brookings Institution, 1995), p. 9.

49 Ibid., p. 10.

50 "Improving America's Schools Act of 1994, Title I—Amendments to the Elementary and Secondary Education Act of 1965." Retrieved from www.ed.gov/legislation/ESEA /sec1001.html on February 3, 2009. The legislation is quoted by Andrew Porter, "The Uses and Misuses of Opportunity-to-Learn Standards," in *Debating the Future of American Education: Do We Need National Standards and Assessments?* edited by Diane Ravitch, pp. 38–67 (Washington, DC: Brookings Institution, 1995), p. 41.

51 As an example of how long the attempt has been made in the courts to achieve equality of spending between school districts, check Richard Lehne's now-dated book, *The Quest for Justice: The Politics of School Finance Reform* (New York: Longman, 1978). Jonathan Kozol's *Savage Inequalities* reinforced the concern about financial inequalities between school districts.

52 Porter, "The Uses and Misuses," p. 41.

53 Wendy Schwartz, "Opportunity to Learn Standards: Impact on Urban Students," ERIC Identifier: ED389816 (New York: ERIC Clearing- House on Urban Education, 1995). Retrieved from www.ericdigests.org/1996-3/urban.htm on February 3, 2009.

54 "2016 Democratic Party platform," p. 30.

55 William J. Clinton, "Inaugural Address," American Presidency Project Document Archive, January 20, 1997, p. 4. Retrieved from www.presidency.ucsb.edu/ws/print.php?pid=54183 on February 3, 2009.

56 "The Gore Agenda: Revolutionizing American Education in the 21st Century," Retrieved from www.gore2000.org on October 3, 2000.

57 John Kerry and John Edwards, *Our Plan for America: Stronger at Home, Respected in the World* (New York: Public Affairs, 2004).

58 Democrats for Education Reform, "Racing to the Top: American Recovery and Reinvestment Act Issues Brief Series #4: World Class Standards and Assessments," June 17, 2009, p. 4." Retrieved from www.dfer.org/Top4/Race_to_Top_4.pdf on February 21, 2013.

59 Ibid., p. 3.

60 Ibid., p. 5.

61 U.S. Department of Education, "Race to the Top Program: Executive Summary. . . ," p. 2.

62 "Mission Statement," Common Core State Standards Initiate. Retrieved from www.corestandards.org/resources/key-points-in-english-language-arts on March 2, 2013.

63 FairTest, "Just Say No to the Test." Retrieved from www.fairtest.org/get-involved/opting-out on January 14, 2017.

64 "2016 Democratic Party platform," p. 33.

65 Ibid., p. 33.

66 Ibid.

67 Hillary Clinton, "K-12 Education." Retrieved from www.hillaryclinton.com/issues/k-12-education/ on January 15, 2017.

68 Ibid.

69 Ibid.

70 David L. Kirp, "Making Schools Work," *New York Times*, May 19, 2012. Retrieved from www.nytimes.com/2012/05/20/opinion/sunday/integration-worked-why-have-we-rejected-it.html?_r=0 on March 27, 2013.

71 Gary Orfield, John Kucsera and Genevieve Siegel-Hawley, "E Pluribus . . . Deepening Double Segregation for More Students," UCLA Civil Rights Project, September 2012. Retrieved from www.civilrightsproject.ucla.edu/research/k-12-education/integration-and-diversity/mlk-national/e-pluribus...separation-deepening-double-segregation-for-more-students?searchterm=E+Pluribus+.+.+.+Deepening+Double+Segregation+for+More+Students on March 27, 2013.

72 Ibid., p. 7.

73 Ibid., p. 9.

74 Ibid., p. 77.

75 Ibid., p. 79–80.

4

BANKS, INVESTMENT FIRMS AND THE EDUCATION BUSINESS

> [T]he truth is that the largest funders of the "reform" movement are the oppo-
> site of disinterested altruists. They are cutthroat businesspeople making shrewd
> financial investments in a movement that is less about educating children than
> about helping "reform" funders hit pay dirt.[1]

The No Child Left Behind legislation and Democratic President Barack Obama's Race to the Top resulted in investment companies and the education industry expanding work in schools. As noted in Chapter 1, there were investment opportunities with the growth of for-profit charter schools—supported by Republicans but rejected by Democrats.

Banks and loan collectors were already handling massive college student loans. The extent of the student loan problem was noted in the 2016 Democratic platform: "Providing Relief from Crushing Student Debt—As we make college affordable for future students, we will not forget about the millions of borrowers with unsustainable levels of student debt, who need help right now."[2] In addition, there were scandals regarding the servicing of student debt. In 2017, the Consumer Financial Protection Bureau sued Navient, "the nation's largest servicer of student loans, has for years misled borrowers and made serious mistakes at nearly every step of the collections process, illegally driving up loan repayment costs for millions of borrowers."[3]

During confirmation hearings for Republican Secretary of Education Betsy DeVos, Democrats raised issues about her income from student loans. The tangle of her financial interests included servicing student loans as reported by the *Washington Post*: "Education Secretary nominee Betsy DeVos and her husband have extensive financial holdings through their private investment and management firm, RDV Corporation. . . . RDV is affiliated with LMF WF Portfolio, a limited liability corporation listed in regulatory filings as one of several firms involved in a $147 million loan to Performant Financial Corp., a debt collection agency in business with the Education Department."[4] According to the Performant Financial Corporation website, they entered the student loan business in 1990 when, "Awarded contract for recovery on defaulted federally-sponsored and funded student loans."[5]

The financial interests tied to student loans are indicative of the complicated nature of the education business. I will begin by discussing the investment companies and the education industry and then turn to the issue of student loans.

Race to the Top: Opening the Door to Investment Firms

Some investment firms and for-profit education industries backed Race to the Top because its agenda promised increased earnings. In addition, members of the Democrats for Education Reform, the political group that shaped Race to the Top policies, came from the investment industry. One of the three founding members of Democrats for Education Reform, John Petry, graduated from the prestigious University of Pennsylvania's Wharton School of Finance and in 2005, when the Democrats for Education Reform was founded, he was a partner at Gotham Capital where he remained until 2010.[6] The United Federation of Teachers, New York City's teachers union and critic of the Race to the Top agenda, provided this description of Petry as a board member of Democrats for Education Reform:"John Petry, a partner at Gotham Capital Management, chairs the board of Education Reform Now. Petry's Gotham Capital LLC, founded in 1985 with $7 million from junk-bond king Michael Milken, is a privately-owned hedge fund that manages investments for wealthy clients, investing in equities as well as spin-offs, restructuring and takeovers."[7]

Whitney Tilson, another founder of Democrats for Education Reform, attended Stanford's Bing Nursery School and the private Northfield Mt. Hermon School in Mount Hermon, Massachusetts. He graduated from Harvard College in 1989 and the Harvard Business School in 1994. He co-founded the Value Investment Congress described as, "the place for value investors from around the world to network with other serious, sophisticated value investors and benefit from the sharing of investment wisdom."[8] As founder and member of the Board of Directors of Democrats for Education Reform, their website describes him as: "Whitney Tilson—Managing Partner, T2 Partners LLC and Tilson Mutual Funds; Board member of KIPP-NYC, National Alliance for Public Charter Schools and Council of Urban Professionals; Co-Founder of the Initiative for a Competitive Inner City and Rewarding Achievement (REACH)."[9]

Ravenal Boykin Curry, the third co-founder of Democrats for Education Reform, was described on their website: "Boykin Curry—Eagle Capital; Co-Founder of Public Prep."[10] It was at Curry's apartment that the Democrats for

Education Reform met with Senator Barack Obama in 2005 to discuss education policy.[11] Steven Brill describes him as a "typical preppie socialite" who "went to Yale and Harvard Business School . . . [and] the regular memos on the economy that he sends his investors, [shows] Curry's interest in education reform was serious and sophisticated."[12]

In evaluating motives behind the Democrat's Race to the Top, it is important to understand the perspective on public schools held by its promoters. By and large, most of the original supporters and implementers of Race to the Top had little public school experience as students, teachers or administrators. Many attended private schools. Why do the sponsors think Race to the Top will improve the quality of American public schools? Embedded in Race to the Top appears to be a disdain of:

1. traditional public schools (let's have charter schools),
2. locally prepared school curricula (without any research, Common Core State Standards are supposed to be an improvement),
3. public school teachers and administrators (value-added testing, again without longitudinal research, is supposed to improve quality of public school teachers and administrators), and
4. college teacher education programs (considered intellectual slumming).

All of the original promoters of Race to the Top attended Ivy League colleges, mostly Harvard. Many were associated with investment banking. In other words, when examining the educational backgrounds of the advocates of Race to the Top it is easy to conclude that they have an elite perspective on public schools.

Consider the educational background of the main spokesperson for Race to the Top, President Obama's U.S. Secretary of Education Arne Duncan. He is private school educated, a graduate of Harvard in sociology, and a professional basketball player[13] Born November 6, 1964, he attended and graduated from the private University of Chicago Laboratory Schools and then went to Harvard majoring in sociology. At Harvard, Duncan co-captained the varsity basketball team and from 1987 to 1991 played professional basketball in Australia. In 1992, a childhood friend and investment banker John W. Rogers, Jr., appointed Duncan director of the Ariel Education Initiative, a mentoring program for children inner-city children. After the school closed in 1996, Duncan and Rogers were instrumental in re-opening it as a charter school, the Ariel Community Academy. In 1999, Duncan was appointed Deputy Chief of Staff for Chicago Public Schools and in 2001 became Chief Executive Officer of the Chicago Public Schools. He held this position until being appointed Secretary of Education in 2008.[14]

It's hard to explain Duncan's rapid rise from professional basketball player to head of the Chicago school system after only 8 years running a mentoring program and working in a charter school. One possible explanation could be the support of investment banker John W. Rogers, Jr., who possibly shared the same ideological views as the investment bankers that formed the Democrats for Education Reform. It's important to note that Duncan did not have any education or experience to even qualify as a school principal let alone CEO of the entire Chicago Public School System.

The goals of the Ariel Community Academy seemed to reflect the perspective of investment bankers about what children from low-income families need. "We want to make the stock market a topic of dinner table conversation," proclaimed a headline splashed across the page of a brochure for the Ariel Community Academy serving students from low-income Chicago families. Duncan continued to support the school after becoming Chief Executive Officer of the Chicago Public Schools and he continued to serve on the school's Board of Directors.[15]

Ironically, at the time of the 2008 collapse of several U.S. investment institutions, including Lehman Brothers, whose personnel spent time at the Academy working as part of the Saturday Morning Teacher Corps, the Ariel Community Academy used an investment curriculum in which "students study commerce, trade and the growth of business around the world." First graders were given $20,000 to invest in a class stock portfolio.[16] Each graduating class was to return the original $20,000 investment to the entering first grade and donate half the profits to the school with the rest distributed among the graduating students.[17]

Embedded in the philosophy of Ariel Community Academy was the human capital argument that education could end poverty. The very actions of the school seemed to indicate that if children from low-income families learned to invest they would be able to escape poverty. On the website for Ariel Investments, their charter school is described as "unique corporate-family-school partnership . . . where financial literacy is not just taught but practiced."[18] If anything, the financial collapse of 2008 may have taught these low-income students to not trust investment bankers or the stock market.

Even President Barack Obama had little experience with public schools. He attended a private elite school and Ivy League colleges. Except for a brief period attending a public school in Honolulu before moving to Indonesia at the age of six, President Obama never attended a public school or taught in one. After returning from Indonesia in 1971, he entered fifth grade at the exclusive Hawaiian private school Punahou graduating in 1979. He then attended Occidental and Columbia University before going on to Harvard Law School where he graduated magna cum laude in 1991.[19] There is little, if nothing, in his educational background to help him understand the inner workings of public schools.

Under Democrat President Obama, limited public school experience seemed to be championed for those entering public school leadership positions. For instance, Joel Klein was a lawyer before being appointed Chancellor of the New York City school system. Unlike those discussed so far in this section, Klein actually attended public schools graduating from William Cullen Bryant High School in Queens, New York in 1963 and then attended Columbia University and Harvard Law School, where he earned his law degree in 1971. He clerked in federal courts and worked in the White House Counsel's under President Clinton. He then became Counsel to Bertelsmann before being appointed by New York City's Mayor Michael Bloomberg to be Chancellor of the New York schools.[20]

Klein, along with his future replacement, Hearst Corporation executive Cathleen Black appointed Chancellor in 2010, had no professional educational background and lacked the legal requirements to head the New York City schools. Mayor Michael Bloomberg explained why he would be a good choice despite Klein's limited school experience, "He has the leadership skills. He has the intergovernmental skills. He has the feeling and compassion for people. He is incorruptible. He is a visionary. And I believe that he will deliver to this city what we promised, a quality education for all of our children."[21] The New York Times reported, "Because Mr. Klein has no experience in school administration, a waiver will be required from the Department of Education in Albany. But Mr. Bloomberg said he was confident that the waiver would be granted. 'If the scholarship and background requirements that Joel Klein has doesn't pass,' the mayor said, 'nobody would pass.'"

Probably nothing better expresses elitist views about schools then Mayor Bloomberg's appointment of Cathleen Black as Chancellor. Her major accomplishment was pioneering the publication of *USA Today* for the Hearst Corporation. Reporter Jeremy Peters noted that, "Schools Chief Has Much in Common With Boss," because of her background as the head of Hearst Corporation's magazine division since 1979.[22] It was reported that she "moved in the same Upper East Side [New York City] circles as the billionaire mayor" and, it could be assumed, the founders of Democrats for Education Reform.[23] She admitted that she wasn't qualified for the position: "A day after her surprise ouster as New York City's top education official, Cathleen P. Black acknowledged that she was ill-prepared for the demands and visibility of running the nation's largest public school system. 'It was like having to learn Russian in a weekend,' Ms. Black said, 'and then give speeches in Russian and speak Russian in budget committee and City Council meetings.'"[24] She lasted only three months and gained some fame for responding to parents' concerns about crowded schools with the quip, "Could we just have some birth control for a while?"[25]

Race to the Top sparked among investment firms. The Education Industries Association, the lobbying group for for-profit education companies, distributed two papers, among many, calling for greater investment in the education sector. One was written for the American Enterprise Institute (AEI), an organization dedicated to promoting the free market economics. The essay was part of the AEI Future of American Education Project. It was titled "Private Capital and Public Education: Toward Quality At Scale"[26] and written by Tom Vander Ark, who was a managing partner of the investment firm LearnCapital and, prior to that, Executive Director of Education for the ubiquitous Bill & Melinda Gates Foundation, which was a major funder of many of the parts of the Race to the Top.[27] The investment portfolio of LearnCapital listed 28 for-profit education companies.[28]

Ark's essay was accompanied by a foreword by Frederick M. Hess, Director of Education Policy Studies at American Enterprise Institute, stressing the role of for-profit companies in achieving the goals of Race to the Top. Hess asserted that schools would improve with "the importance of for-profit education companies that can attract venture capital and that are better equipped to sustain and grow through profits and private equity."[29]

Ark used a similar argument that government spending has been wasted by being channeled through a rigid education bureaucracy. To bring about real change, he asserted, required the involvement of for-profit education industries funded by venture capital. In his words,

> While the public delivery system is inflexible and bureaucratic and provides an inadequate impetus for performance and improvement, non-profit organizations have weak incentives and limited ability to aggregate capital for research and development or scaled impact. In contrast, for-profit enterprises may have greater ability to attract talent and capital, incentives to achieve scaled impact, and the ability to utilize multiple business strategies.[30]

In the context of the changes advocated in Race to the Top, he wrote, "Private capital and for-profit enterprises will play a vital role in creating tools that increase learning, staffing, and facilities productivity."[31]

Besides justifying for-profit education industries with claims that public school bureaucracies were inflexible, investment groups warned that about the power of teachers unions and asserted that school reform would solve the problem of increasing inequality of incomes. An example of this argument can be found in a long, 332 pages, investment report distributed by the Education Industry Association and published by GSV Capital with the title: *American Revolution 2.0: How Education Innovation is Going to Revitalize and Transform the U.S. Economy.*[32] The lead author of the report is Michael Moe, co-founder of GSV Capital and its Chief Investment Officer. The company's website describes him:

> Michael is well known and regarded as one of the world's preeminent authorities on growth investing. *His insights are routinely solicited by everyone from CNBC to Barron's to Congress.* Recognized as one of the best and brightest investors on Wall Street, his honors include *Institutional Investor's* All American' research team, *The Wall Street Journal's* 'Best on the Street' award, and being named by *Business Week* as 'one of the best stock pickers in the country.'[33]

The basic argument of American Revolution 2.0 was that improving schools depended on greater involvement of the for-profit education sector. This would result, it was stated, in the American economy being revitalized and income inequalities reduced.

The report conveyed a fear that inequality of income would lead to some form of revolution—a revolution that they claim can be countered by an "education" revolution. The report asserted, "Occupy Wall Street (OWS) and adjacent uprisings have powerfully demonstrated that a large and growing segment of American society doesn't believe that they are participating in the future. . . . Aristotle observed, 'Inequality is the parent of revolution.'"[34] The report listed major revolutions from the 1910 Mexican Revolution to 2010 Arab Spring and on the page listing the revolutions was a photo of a Occupy Wall Street protester holding a sign, "One day the poor will have nothing left to eat but the rich."[35]

Of course, being a capital investment firm, the report didn't advocate redistribution of wealth: "Joe the Plumber is right in that redistribution of wealth is not a sustainable economic philosophy, nor is it an American one."[36] They argued that using the tax system to reduce income inequalities could result in spreading "the seeds of class chaos [which] could easily result in a Robin Hood State instead of addressing the real issue of preparing people to be productive in the world we are in."[37] The real revolution, the report suggests, should be against the public schools: "The revolution America needs today is not against an oppressive monarchy, but rather *against an education system that has equally oppressive effects* [author's emphasis]."[38]

Using the metaphors of war and revolution, the report called for a "Second American Revolution" declaring that they have the "arms and technology to fight this war."[39] This revolution would be led by for-profit technology companies providing learning products to schools. The "battlefield" was described as the "Unions" and "Status Quo Forces" versus "Change Agents." Showing a photo of an 18th-century American revolutionary soldier, the status quo forces are given as:

1. Unions and beneficiaries of current system
2. Tenure
3. No choice, no competition
4. For-profits for the enemy
5. Transparency is avoided.[40]

Fighting against the status quo, the report presented what it called the "Arms Dealers."[41] These "arms dealers" were for-profit education companies, which the report presented as investment opportunities. First on the list was Rupert Murdoch's News Corporation's Education Division offering a now failed product Amplify accompanied by the note: "Recently rebranded 'Amplify' educational services division partnering with AT&T to provide purpose-built tablets and develop other digital learning platforms for K-12 Classrooms."[42] Second recommended investment was Pearson, a major player in textbook publishing and testing, which the report notes: "Recent acquisitions of Schoolnet and TutorVista dramatically expand digital instruction footprint. . . . Continued investments/partnerships with Knewton, Tabula Digita, Inkling, and Florida Virtual support scared grow in digital learning."[43] Knewton is a pioneer in applying analytics to large data sets. The other "arms dealers" are Macmillan, McGraw-Hill, Cengage Learning, Houghton Mifflin Harcourt, Scholastic, Blackboard, Dell, Apple and Microsoft.[44]

Encouraged by the Race to the Top agenda, both *American Revolution 2.0* and the American Enterprise essay "Private Capital and Public Education: Toward Quality At Scale" endorsed investments in for-profit education companies. There was money to be made selling products to fulfill the Race to the Top, such as analytic education platforms, software and services to help use the data for "value-added" teacher and principal evaluations, and providing services to help integrate the Common Core State Standards into local curricula.

The Common Core State Standards resulted in an avalanche of books and software programs to help local schools implement the standards.[45] And, of course, for-profit charter school-management companies benefited from the Race to the Top's call to increase the number of charter schools. Regarding profits to be earned from charter schools, the National Education Policy Center reported in 2012 that: "The number of states in which for-profit EMOs operated was 33 in 2010–2011. The for-profit education management industry expanded into Alaska and Hawaii this past year for the first time. Only one Alaska and one Hawaii school were fully managed by a for-profit EMO during this period."[46] The report identified the leading for-profit companies operating charter schools and managing public schools:

> This year, after the acquisition of KC Distance Learning, K12's total enrollment for its 49 schools (65,396) far exceeds any other EMO. National Heritage Academies' 67 schools come in a far second, with a total enrollment of 42,503. An early leader in the education management industry, EdisonLearning, has slipped to fourth in terms of total enrollment, behind Imagine Schools, Inc.[47]

In summary, investors could make money from every aspect of Race to the Top.

Common Core State Standards: Making Money in New York

Common Core State Standards generated profits for many companies. For instance, the New York State Board of Regents in 2013 purchased for $28,335,642 English/Language Arts and mathematics curricula aligned with the Common Core State Standards.[48] The PreK-2 English/Language curriculum was purchased from the Core Knowledge Foundation, an organization run by E.D. Hirsch, Jr.[49] The English/Language curriculum for grades 3–5 was purchased from Expeditionary Learning and for grades 6–8 from Expeditionary Learning under a subcontract with Public Consulting Group. Expeditionary Learning describes itself: "We partner with schools, districts, and charter boards to open new schools and transform existing schools. We provide school leaders and teachers with professional development, curriculum planning resources, and new school structures to boost student engagement, character, and achievement."[50] In 2010, Expeditionary Learning reported working in or running 165 schools in 29 states and Washington, DC.[51]

The Public Consulting Group is an example of a company created primarily to exploit government spending for human services. Besides subcontracting the Expeditionary Learning curriculum, the company also sold to New York the English/Language Arts for grades 9–12.[52] The company describes its services: "Public Consulting Group (PCG) provides industry-leading management consulting and technology to help public sector education, health, human services, and other government clients achieve their performance goals and better serve populations in need."[53] Besides selling restructuring services, the company is benefiting from the Common Core State Standards by selling aligned curriculum packages.

In summary, there was money to be made off Race to the Top.

Human Capital and Economists: Alternative Teacher Certification and Evaluation

Democratic reliance on human capital theory was used in the Race to the Tops' search for alternative teacher education certification and teacher evaluation methods. Economists Harvard Professor Thomas Kane and Hoover Institute's Eric Hanushek questioned the value of teacher education programs and public school evaluations systems. As I discussed in Chapter 3, human capital economists are behind most of the rhetoric that changing public schools will improve the U.S. economy and make the U.S. more competitive against other global economies. I asserted in Chapter 3 that despite claims of human capital economists, there is no longitudinal research that convincingly shows changing schools will improve America's ability to compete in world markets or reduce inequality of incomes.

An example of these kinds of economic assertions can be found in a report crucial to the Race to the Top's agenda for value-added teaching and alternatives to traditional teacher certification. The Democrats for Education Reform placed their party in conflict with the teachers' unions by calling for changes in teacher tenure, credentialing and merit pay. Reflecting this changed focus was the influential 2006 Brooking Institute's Hamilton project report *Identifying Effective Teachers: Using Performance on the Job.*[54]

The Hamilton Project report dismissed traditional methods of teacher credentialing based on a specified set of college courses and passing a test. The report cited studies that showed there was little difference in quality between credentialed and non-credentialed teachers. As a result, the report advocated increasing alternative routes to teaching.[55]

> Recommendation 1: Reduce the barriers to entry into teaching for those without traditional teacher certification. The evidence suggests that there

is no reason to limit initial entrance into teaching to those who have completed traditional certification programs or are willing to take such courses in their first years on the job."[56]

The second and third recommendations called for making it harder for teachers to get tenure and to provide bonuses for highly effective teachers in schools serving low-income students.

What would prove to be the most controversial of the proposals, putting Democrats in conflict with the teachers' unions, was the fourth recommendation for evaluating teachers based on how much an individual teacher raised class test scores. The report did not call for abandoning traditional measures, such as observations and principal evaluations, but called for "some measure of 'value-added,' or the average gain in performance for students assigned to each teacher." One of the authors of the report, the previously mentioned Harvard Professor Thomas Kane, was a champion of using "value-added" methods for teacher evaluation. In the previously stated recommendation of bonuses for "effective" teachers in low-income schools, the word "effective" refers to raising student test scores.

Similar to our previous discussion of investor reports, the Hamilton Project claims, that "education has become a constraint on future productivity growth and a root cause of income inequality."[57] There is no footnote or other citation provided for this assertion!

The Hamilton report's authors, Robert Gordon, Thomas J. Kane and Douglas Staiger, are all economists who were part of a network linked to the Democrats for Educational Reform. At the time of the report's publication, Robert Gordon was Senior Vice President for Economic Policy, Center for American Progress and Associate Director for Education, Income Maintenance and Labor in the Office of Budget and Management.[58] Douglas Staiger was an economist at Dartmouth College.[59] And most importantly, the third author and pioneer in the work of value-added evaluations of teachers was Thomas Kane a Professor of Education and Economics at the Harvard Graduate School of Education and a faculty member at the Kennedy School of Government.[60]

Their economic arguments that the root cause of income inequality and claims that higher levels of credentialing were required by the labor market were not supported by employment projections of the U.S. Bureau of Labor statistics. In fact, those interpreting the statistics might conclude that increased educational levels of the population might result in educational inflation or brain waste, such as college graduates being unemployed or working as waiters and cooks. The U.S. Bureau of Labor Statistics' Occupational Outlook Handbook states for the period 2010–2020 that: "Total employment is expected to increase by 20.5 million jobs from 2010 to 2020, with 88 percent of detailed occupations projected to experience employment growth. Industries and occupations related to *health care, personal care and social assistance, and construction* are projected to have the fastest job growth between 2010 and 2020 [author's emphasis]."[61] According to their projections the top two fastest growing occupations, personal care aides and home health aides, require: "Entry-level Education: Less than high school."[62] The next fastest growing job sector "Medical Secretaries" requires a high school diploma or equivalent. In 2013, the National Association of Home Builders announced:

> March 21, 2013—Growing labor shortages in all facets of the residential construction sector are impeding the housing and economic recovery, according to a new survey conducted by the National Association of Home Builders (NAHB). The survey of our members shows that since June of 2012, residential construction firms are reporting an increasing number of shortages in all aspects of the industry—from carpenters, excavators, framers, roofers and plumbers, to bricklayers, HVAC, building maintenance managers and weatherization workers.[63]

According to the Bureau of Labor Statistics, these jobs require less than a high school diploma or a high school diploma or its equivalent.[64]

The Hamilton report's assertion, without any supporting reference, that education is the solution to income inequality is similar to that of previously discussed investment reports. It seems like more of a hope than based on any realities of the job market. A similar issue arises when they report on the differences between teachers with and without teaching credentials. This was a key argument in the criticism of teacher training programs and the push for alternative forms of certification.

The three economists asserted: "Controlling for baseline characteristics of students and comparing classrooms within schools, there is no statistically significant difference in achievement for students assigned to certified and uncertified teachers."[65] Based on this assertion, they argue, "that there is no reason to limit initial entrance into teaching to those who have completed traditional certification programs or are willing to take such courses in their first years on the job."[66]

The citation for the claim of no statistical difference between certified and noncertified teachers is an unpublished paper.[67] This unpublished paper was limited to two cohorts of elementary school teachers hired by the Los Angeles school district in the 1995–96 and 1996–97 school year when many uncertified teachers were being hired because of a teacher shortage. The authors' conclusion used the word "suggesting" and not "proof" in comparing teacher effectiveness: "The absence of any impact on student achievement is consistent with our cross-sectional results, *suggesting* certified teachers were no more effective than the uncertified [author's emphasis]."[68] Student test scores were used to evaluate teacher effectiveness. However, they eliminated from the study students who switched teachers during the course of a year, students with disabilities, and students in "classrooms with extraordinarily large (more than 36) or extraordinarily small (less than 10)."[69]

Besides cherry-picking the students, a closer look at their results suggest that credentialed teachers performed better than noncredentialled teachers. For example, they found: "Within a given school, grade, calendar track and academic year, the students assigned to less experienced and uncertified teachers appear to perform poorly relative to those assigned to traditionally certified teachers."[70]

Not to belabor the point, it does seem odd that an unpublished research study based on two school years in one city would result in a conclusion that being a credentialed teacher made no difference in student learning and resulted in a policy recommendation to, "Reduce the barriers to entry into teaching for those without traditional teacher certification."[71]

The 2006 Hamilton Project's "Identifying Effective Teachers Using Performance on the Job" continues to be cited to justify value-added and alternative forms of certification. For instance, Michelle Rhee's The New Teacher Project, formed in 1997 with Teach for America, continues to cite the 2006 study. Their 2010 report "Teacher Evaluation 2.0" has on its opening page a quote from the Hamilton Project's study: "Having a top-quartile teacher rather than a bottom-quartile teacher four years in a row could be enough to close the black-white test score gap. Gordon, Kane and Staiger, 2006."[72] Among several evaluation methods, the report proposes: "Whenever possible, these should include objective measures of student academic growth, such as value-added models that connect students' progress on standardized assessments to individual teachers while controlling for important factors such as students' academic history."[73]

The claim, embodied in President Obama's education policies, that teacher evaluation was key to reducing the disparity in "black-white" test scores and inequalities of income, matched concerns found in the previously discussed investment reports. It shifts the causality of economic problems, inequalities of income and economic growth, to the public schools. By presenting this argument it counters the possibility of changing the tax system or other government policies to reduce income disparities. It also protects wealthier public school districts from plans for economic integration of poor and wealthy school districts by claiming schools serving low-income students will improve through changes in teacher credentialing and evaluation.

The Student Loan Crises

By the 2016 election, college student loans were a national crisis. Banks and collecting agencies were making a fortune from student loans, which, as I will describe, had none of the consumer protections of other loans. Many students couldn't keep up with payments, which resulted in defaults that earned lenders more money than if students paid off their loans.[74]

As mentioned at the beginning of this chapter, the 2016 Democratic platform advocated relief from, in its words, crushing student debt. During the 2016 campaign, Hillary Clinton declared: "Let's . . . make debt-free college available to everyone. . . . And let's liberate the millions of Americans who already have student debt."[75] The 2016 Democratic platform and Hillary Clinton proposed debt-free higher education in the context of economic goals: "Democrats believe that in America, if you want a higher education, you should always be able to get one: money should never stand in the way. . . . Bold new investments by the federal government, coupled with states reinvesting in higher education and colleges holding the line on costs, *will ensure that Americans of all backgrounds will be prepared for the jobs and economy of the future* [author's emphasis]."[76]

There were two methods for dealing with the student loan issue. One was to return to a pre-1970s period, when public universities and colleges had lower tuition fees and only required students to find small amounts of other money for support.[77] The other method was to revamp the whole student loan industry.

In 2016, Democrats advocated both approaches. One was to call for free tuition at state universities and community colleges. Democratic candidate Hillary Clinton declared: "Every student should have the option to graduate from a public college or university in their state without taking on any student debt. By 2021, families with income up to $125,000 will pay no tuition at in-state four-year public colleges and universities."[78] In addition, she offered immediate tuition relief: "And from the beginning, every student from a family making $85,000 a year or less will be able to go to an in-state four-year public college or university without paying tuition. All community colleges will offer free tuition."[79]

To reduce the cost of college, the 2016 Democratic platform called for, "Bold new investments by the federal government, coupled with states reinvesting in higher education and colleges holding the line on costs. We will also make community college free, while ensuring the strength of our Historically Black Colleges and Universities and Minority-Serving Institutions."[80]

Proposals for student loan relief tackled the decline in consumer protections since the 1965 Higher Education Act provided loan guarantees to banks that lended to students. In 1972, federal legislation established the Student Loan Marketing Association (Sallie Mae). The purpose of Sallie Mae was to purchase student loans made by banks as a means of encouraging greater lending. In 1997, Sallie Mae was privatized and began making loans directly to students. It also began to purchase other companies involved in the student loan business. Banks also issued their own student loans.

Defaults on student loans proved highly profitable. The 1998 Amendments to the Higher Education Act allowed lenders to charge large penalties and fees for student loan defaults. Lenders could take up to 25 percent of each dollar paid on defaulted student loans without applying it to principal and interest. Also, the legislation removed statutes of limitation on student loans—you could never escape your student loan debt except in death. Some students were trapped in ever increasing debt as penalties and fees were added to their defaulted loans. The 2005 Bankruptcy Abuse Prevention and Consumer Protection Act made "all student loans . . . nondischargeable in bankruptcy."[81] In other words, you would still owe your student loan debt even after bankruptcy. Also, there are no mechanisms for refinancing your loan at another lender or at a lower interest rate.

Students who defaulted on their loans were potentially trapped in a lifetime of debt that kept increasing because of penalties and fees. Lenders were given free rein by Congressional legislation to pursue aggressive tactics loan collection tactics. In the words of Alan Michael Collinge, "These powers [of collection] included wage, Social Security, and disability garnishment, as well as tax seizure, suspension of state-issued professional licenses, and the termination of public employment."[82]

As mentioned previously, Republican Secretary of Education Betsy DeVos encountered nomination problems because of her investments in Performant Financial Corp. The 2016 Republican platform called for privatization of student loans: "The federal government should not be in the business of originating student loans. In order to bring down college costs and give students access to a multitude of financing options, private sector participation in student financing should be restored."[83]

President Obama's administration provided some relief by offering a repayment plan based on income. As the U.S. Department of Education states: "If your federal student loan payments are high compared to your income, you may want to repay your loans under an income-driven repayment plan. *Most federal student loans are eligible for at least one income-driven repayment plan. If your income is low enough, your payment could be as low as $0 per month*."[84]

However, student loan collection companies were not too happy with the new repayment plan as evidenced by a front-page headline of the *New York Times*: "*Student Loan Collector Cheated Millions, Lawsuits Say*."[85] The article featured Navient, purportedly the country's largest servicer of student loans, who either steered payees away from Obama's repayment plan or failed to mention that it had to be renewed each year. In 2014, Navient split off from Sallie Mae. Handling $300 billion in private and federal loans for 12 million borrowers, Navient doesn't initiate loans but acts as a collection agency.

According to the *New York Times*, the Consumer Financial Protection Bureau claimed Navient deliberately steered "borrowers away from income-based repayment plans that could have lowered their loan costs—in order to maximize its own profits. Enrolling customers in such plans can be time-consuming and complex, and Navient's compensation system for its customer service representatives encouraged them to push struggling customers toward other options."[86] In addition, the company failed to tell those using the income-based repayment plans that they had to be renewed each year. Often the company suggested that borrowers select "loan forbearance" over the income-based repayment plan. Loan forbearance suspends payments but allows the continued accumulation of interest on a loan.

One example provided by the *New York Times* was of Andrew Brittle who took out multiple loans to attend DeVry a for-profit school. Currently, Brittell, with a family of five, works in the billing department of a telecommunications company for $3,000 a month after taxes. He qualified for the income-based repayment plan. However, when he applied to Navient the company "repeatedly lost his paperwork, and each time, Navient suggested that Mr. Brittell instead apply for yet another loan forbearance. . . . Mr. Brittell's loans have been in forbearance for more than five years. He has made no payments on them, and the balance due has ballooned to more than $90,000."[87] In another example, a Ms. Vitakauskas borrowed approximately $50,000 to earn a degree in English. It took her 6 years to get a repayment plan. By then the loan with interest and penalties had grown to $100,000.[88]

Even the disabled and elderly face continued problems with Navient. Technically, those with a "total and permanent" disability are forgiven their student loans. However, "Navient improperly marked some of those charged-off loans as defaults, the bureau said, leaving those borrowers, including disabled soldiers, with black marks on their credit records that could have prevented them from obtaining mortgages and other loans."[89] In addition, 2.8 million Americans over 60 in 2017 had outstanding student debt.[90] As noted earlier, student loan collection companies have the right to garnish Social Security payments.

Leading the complaints, as I will discuss in the next chapter, was Democratic candidate Bernie Sanders. Many of his concerns appeared in the 2016 Democratic platform and in Hillary Clinton's campaign messages. The 2016 platform promised to reverse past legislation that kept student borrowers from refinancing their debts at a lower rate and bankruptcy laws. "Democrats will allow those who currently have student debt to refinance their loans at the lowest rates possible. . . . Democrats will restore the prior standard in bankruptcy law to allow borrowers with student loans to be able to discharge their debts in bankruptcy as a measure of last resort."[91] The platform also promised to simplify the process for applying for income-based repayment plans.

Hillary Clinton's campaign also supported the right to refinance student loans and proposed a limit on payments of 10 percent of income: "Borrowers will be able to refinance loans at current rates, providing debt relief to an estimated 25 million people. They'll never have to pay back more than 10 percent of their income, and all remaining college debt will be forgiven after 20 years."[92] She also promised help for those in default: "Delinquent borrowers and those in default will get help to protect their credit and get back on their feet."[93]

Besides promising to reduce interest rates on student loans, Clinton proposed something that may have struck fear in the student loan industry: "Hillary will take immediate executive action to offer a three-month moratorium on student loan payments to all federal loan borrowers. That will give every borrower a chance to consolidate their loans, sign up for income-based repayment plans, and take advantage of opportunities to reduce their monthly interest payments and fees."[94]

The day after Republican President Donald Trump was sworn into office, MarketWatch reporter Jillian Berman proclaimed: "Investors are cheering student loan stocks ahead of President Trump-Will bets on Sallie Mae, Navient and others pay off?"[95] Berman went on to state: "As President Donald Trump moves into the White House, much remains uncertain about the future of many policy issues, including student debt. But investors appear to be betting that President Trump and Republican Congress will be good for the companies involved in the $1.3 trillion student loan business."[96]

Conclusion

No Child Left Behind and Race to the Top spurred the growth of the education industry and increased the interest of investment firms in education. Mainly drawn from investment firms, Democrats for Education Reform influenced Democratic President Barack Obama's Race to the Top. Many of the supporters of this reform effort did not attend public schools including President Obama's Secretary of Education Arne Duncan. Democrats for Education Reform, President Obama and Arne Duncan supported policies that some might consider anti-teacher and anti-public schools. Race to the Top expanded charter schools as part of a war on poverty rather than focus on public schools. The Democratic reformers didn't trust public schools to develop their own curricula, but relied on the Governor's Association Common Core State Standards. Criticizing public school teachers and administrators, many Democrats supported teacher and principal evaluations based on student test scores, such as value-added student testing, despite the lack of any longitudinal study that this would improve quality of teachers and schools. Alternative routes to teacher certification were promoted despite any research that these alternative routes would provide better teachers as compared to traditional teacher education programs.

In other words, this was an elitist (by elitist in this case I mean wealthy individuals who disdained public education) set of reforms that opened the door to money-making investment firms and education companies. The testing requirements of No Child Left Behind, combined with the Common Core State Standards, channeled public money to the for-profit education industry. Testing alone helped expand the shadow education industry composed of test and tutoring companies like Sylvan Learning, Kaplan, Princeton Review and Kumon. Helping teachers and administrators implement the Common Core State Standards became a major industry.

In 2016, Democrats did try to curb at least one education industry, namely, the student loan industry. However, they lost the election, which may have ensured total privatization of the student loan industry and little, if no relief, from this growing drag on the economy.

As stressed in Chapter 3, Democrats continued to justify their educational efforts by relying on the unproven human capital arguments that increased schooling would end poverty, grow the economy and reduce inequality between incomes. The elitist views of education emerging from the Obama administration were most troubling because they were often embedded in claims of helping the poor. Race to the Top was a major, I would argue, waste of money and time resulting in little improvement in American education.

Notes

1 David Sirota, "Stop Pretending Wealthy CEOs Pushing for Charter Schools Are Altruistic 'Reformers'. They're Raking in Billions," *Salon.com*. Retrieved from www.salon.com/2013/03/11/getting_rich_off_of_schoolchildren/ on March 12, 2013.

2 "2016 Democratic Party platform," July 21, 2016, p. 31. Retrieved from www.presidency.ucsb.edu/papers_pdf/117717.pdf on January 10, 2017, p. 30.

3 Stacy Cowley and Jessica Silver-Greenberg, "Student Loan Collector Cheated Millions, Lawsuits Say," *New York Times*, January 18, 2017. Retrieved from www.nytimes.com/2017/01/18/business/dealbook/student-loans-navient-lawsuit.html?ref=todayspaper on January 19, 2017.

4 Danielle Douglas-Gabriel, "Dems Raise Concern About Possible Links Between DeVos and Student Debt Collection Agency," *The Washington Post*, January 17, 2017. Retrieved from www.washingtonpost.com/news/grade-point/wp/2017/01/17/dems-raise-concern-about-possible-links-between-devos-and-student-debt-collection-agency/?utm_term=.0146784636a3 on January 19, 2017.

5 Performant Financial Corporation, "History Performant Past and Present." Retrieved from https://performantcorp.com/about-us/history/ on January 19, 2017.

6 LinkedIn, "Profile John Petry." Retrieved from www.linkedin.com/in/john-petry-9a42606 on March 19, 2013.

7 Maisie McAdoo, "Attack of the Hedge-Fund Managers Why Do They Care About Schools? It's All About Money, United Federation of Teachers: New York Teacher Issue," June 3, 2010. Retrieved from www.uft.org/news-stories/attack-hedge-fund-managers on March 19, 2013.

8 Value Investing Congress, "Home." Retrieved from www.valueinvestingcongress.com/ on March 19, 2013.

9 Democrats for Education Reform, "Board of Directors." Retrieved from www.dfer.org/list/about/board/ on March 19, 2013.

10 Ibid.

11 Steven Brill, *Class Warfare: Inside the Fight to Fix America's Schools* (New York: Simon & Schuster, 2011), pp. 131–132.

12 Ibid., p. 116.

13 Ibid., pp. 219–228.

14 See Ibid., pp. 236–244 and U.S. Department of Education, "Senior Staff—Arne Duncan, U.S. Secretary of Education—Biography." Retrieved from http://www2.ed.gov/news/staff/bios/duncan.html on March 18, 2013.

15 "Give Children the Best in Education and Watch Their Potential Grow: Ariel Education Initiative, 2007." Brochure retrieved from Ariel Education Initiative www.arielinvestments.com/content/view/106/1066/ on December 16, 2008.

16 Ibid.

17 Ibid.

18 Ariel Investments, "Ariel Community Academy." Retrieved from www.arielinvestments.com/ariel-community-academy/ on March 18, 2013.

19 Martin Kelly, "Barack Obama—President of the United States." Retrieved from http://americanhistory.about.com/od/biographiesmr/p/barack_obama.htm on March 18, 2013.

20 NYC.gov, "Mayor Michael R. Bloomberg Appoints Joel Klein As Schools Chancellor." Retrieved from www.nyc.gov/portal/site/nycgov/menuitem.b270a4a1d51bb

3017bce0ed101c789a0/index.jsp?pageID=nyc_blue_room&catID=1194&doc_name=http%3A%2F%2Fwww.nyc.gov%2Fhtml%2Fom%2Fhtml%2F2002b%2Fpr201-02.html&cc=unused1978&rc=1194&ndi=1 on March 22, 2013.

21 Jeremy W. Peters, "Schools Chief Has Much in Common With Boss," *New York Times*, November 9, 2010. Retrieved from www.nytimes.com/2010/11/10/nyregion/10black.html?pagewanted=print on March 22, 2013.

22 Ibid.

23 Michael Barbaro, Sharon Otterman, and Javier C. Hernandez, "After 3 Months, Mayor Replaces Schools Leader," *New York Times*, April 7, 2011. Retrieved from www.nytimes.com/2011/04/08/education/08black.html?pagewanted=all on March 22, 2013.

24 Michael Barbaro, "Black Admits Being Ill Prepared," *New York Times*, April 8, 2011. Retrieved from www.nytimes.com/2011/04/09/nyregion/09black.html?pagewanted=print on March 22, 2013.

25 Barbaro, Otterman, and Hernandez, "After 3 Months. . . ."

26 Tom Vander Ark, "Private Capital and Public Education: Toward Quality at Scale," AEI Future of American Education Project Working Paper 2009–02, American Enterprise Institute (Washington, DC: American Enterprise Institute, 2009).

27 LearnCapital, "Team." Retrieved from www.learncapital.com/team/ on March 15, 2013.

28 LearnCapital, "Portfolio." Retrieved from www.learncapital.com/portfolio/ on March 21, 2013.

29 Fredrick M. Hess, "Foreword" to Tom Vander Ark, "Private Capital and Public Education: Toward Quality at Scale," AEI Future of American Education Project Working Paper 2009–02, American Enterprise Institute (Washington, DC: American Enterprise Institute, 2009).

30 Ark, "Private Capital. . . ," p. 1.

31 Ibid.

32 Michael T. Moe, Matthew P. Hanson, Li Jang, and Luben Pampoulov, *American Revolution 2.0: How Education Is Going to Revitalize America and Transform the U.S. Economy* (Woodside, CA: GSV Asset Management, July 4, 2012).

33 GSV Capital, "Management Team." Retrieved from http://gsvcap.com/management/ on March 16, 2013.

34 Moe, *American Revolution 2.0: How Education Is Going . . .*, p. 19, 25.

35 Ibid., p. 24.

36 Ibid., p. 25.

37 Ibid.

38 Ibid.

39 Ibid.

40 Ibid., p. 47.

41 Ibid., p. 48.

42 Ibid.

43 Ibid.

44 Ibid., pp. 48–49.

45 A visit to Amazon's Common Core State Standards page shows the industry created by the Standards, www.amazon.com/s/ref=nb_sb_ss_i_3_17?url=search-alias%3Daps&field-keywords=common+core+state+standards&sprefix=Common+core+state%2Caps%2C125&crid=GCJ81ZQMNMPE.

46 Gary Miron, Jessica L. Urschel, Mayra A. Yat Aguilar, and Breanna Dailey, *Profiles of For-Profit and Nonprofit Education Management Organizations: Thirteenth Annual Report—2010–2011* (Boulder, CO: School of Education, University of Colorado Boulder, January 2012). National Education Policy Center.

47 Ibid., p. ii.

48 Catherine Gewertz, "Educators Questioning Timing of State Tests Reflecting Standards," *Education Week*, March 27, 2013, pp. 1, 14–15.
49 Core Knowledge Foundation, Retrieved from www.coreknowledge.org/.
50 Expeditionary Learning, "Our Approach." Retrieved from http://elschools.org/our-approach April 1, 2013.
51 Expeditonary Learning, "History." Retrieved from http://elschools.org/about-us/history on April 1, 2013.
52 Gewertz, "Educators Questioning. . . ," p. 14.
53 Public Consulting Group, "About." Retrieved from www.publicconsultinggroup.com/about/index.html on April 1, 2013.
54 Robert Gordon, Thomas J. Kane, and Douglas Staiger, *Identifying Effective Teachers Using Performance on the Job* (Washington, DC: The Brookings Institution, 2006).
55 Ibid., p. 7.
56 Ibid., p. 6.
57 Ibid., p. 5.
58 The Hamilton Project, "Author Robert Gordon." Retrieved from www.hamiltonproject.org/about_us/our_people/robert_gordon/ on March 25, 2013.
59 Dartmouth, "Douglas Staiger." Retrieved from www.dartmouth.edu/~dstaiger/pub.html March 25, 2013.
60 Harvard Kennedy School, John F. Kennedy School of Government, "Thomas Kane." Retrieved from www.hks.harvard.edu/about/faculty-staff-directory/thomas-kane on March 25, 2013.
61 United States Department of Labor, Bureau of Labor Statistics, "Occupational Outlook Handbook: Projections Overview." Retrieved from www.bls.gov/ooh/About/Projections-Overview.htm on March 25, 2013.
62 Ibid.
63 National Association of Home Builders, "Growing Labor Shortages Impeding Housing and Economic Recovery." Retrieved from www.nahb.org/news_details.aspx?newsID=15880 on March 25, 2013.
64 United States Department of Labor, Bureau of Labor Statistics, "Occupational Outlook Handbook. . . ."
65 Gordon, Kane, and Staiger, *Identifying Effective Teachers . . .*, p. 6.
66 Ibid., p. 5.
67 "Using Imperfect Information to Identify Effective Teachers." Unpublished Paper. Los Angeles: School of Public Affairs, University of California—Los Angeles.
68 Thomas J. Kane and Douglas O. Staiger, "Using Imperfect Information to Identify Effective Teachers," April 25, 2005. Retrieved from www.dartmouth.edu/~dstaiger/Papers/2005/Kane%20Staiger%20teacher%20quality%204%2028%2005.pdf on March 26, 2013.
69 Ibid., p. 11.
70 Ibid., p. 13.
71 Gordon, Kane, and Staiger, *Identifying Effective Teachers . . .*, p. 6.
72 The New Teacher Project, "Teacher Evaluation 2.0," 2010. Retrieved from http://tntp.org/assets/documents/Teacher-Evaluation-Oct10F.pdf?files/Teacher-Evaluation-Oct10F.pdf on March 27, 2013.
73 Ibid., p. 6.
74 Alan Michael Collinge, *The Student Loan Scam: The Most Oppressive Debt in History—And How We Can Fight Back* (Boston, MA: Beacon Press, 2009).
75 "Making College Debt-Free and Taking on Student Debt," Hillary Clinton Campaign Website. Retrieved from www.hillaryclinton.com/issues/college/ on January 20, 2017.
76 "2016 Democratic Party platform," p. 30.
77 Collinge, *The Student Loan Scam*, p. 4.

78 "2016 Democratic Party platform," p. 30.

79 Ibid.

80 Ibid.

81 Collinge, *The Student Loan Scam*, p. 15.

82 Ibid., p. 17.

83 "Republican platform 2016," p. 35. Retrieved from https://gop.com/platform/ on November 23, 2016.

84 U.S. Department of Education, Federal Student Aid Office. Retrieved from https://studentaid.ed.gov/sa/repay-loans/understand/plans/income-driven on January 23, 2017.

85 Cowley and Silver-Greenberg, "Student Loan Collector Cheated Millions. . . ."

86 Ibid.

87 Stacy Cowley and Jessica Silver-Greenberg, "In Navient Lawsuits, Unsettling Echoes of Past Lending Crisis," *New York Times*, January 19, 2017. Retrieved from www.nytimes.com/2017/01/19/business/dealbook/navient-loans-lawsuit.html?ref=todayspaper&_r=0 on January 23, 2017.

88 Ibid.

89 Cowley and Silver-Greenberg, "Student Loan Collector Cheated Millions. . . ."

90 Ibid.

91 "2016 Democratic Party platform," p. 31.

92 "Making College Debt-Free and Taking on Student Debt," *Hillary Clinton Campaign Website.* . . .

93 Ibid.

94 Ibid.

95 Jillian Berman, "Investors Are Cheering Student Loan Stocks Ahead of President Trump," *MarketWatch*, January 21, 2017. Retrieved from www.marketwatch.com/story/investors-are-cheering-student-loan-stocks-ahead-of-president-trump-2017-01–19 on January 23, 2017.

96 Ibid.

5

THE DEMOCRATIC LEFT, THE GREEN AND LIBERTARIAN PARTIES

In recognition of Bernie Sanders influence and strong following during the 2016 Democratic primary race, I added a new category "Democratic Left" to this edition of *Political Agendas for Education*. Sanders's claim that the U.S. political system was now run by an oligarchy of the wealthy was hailed as an alternative to the usual rhetoric of the Democratic and Republican parties. Sanders concerns about the cost of higher education and student debt directly influenced Hillary Clinton's campaign and the 2016 Democratic platform. As reported by NBC News in July 2016: "Extending an olive branch to Bernie Sanders and his supporters, Hillary Clinton on Wednesday will announce a plan to make in-state public colleges and universities free for students from families who make less than $125,000 a year."[1]

Also, in this Chapter, I will be discussing the Green and Libertarian Parties, which offer strikingly different education agendas from that of Bernie Sanders. The Green Party is the major educational alternative to Republican and Democratic education agendas by emphasizing the environment, educating active and critical thinking citizens and a strong educational arts agenda. On the other hand, the Libertarian Party is closest to the 2016 Republican education agenda and the thinking of Secretary of Education Betsy DeVos, but it did advocate education proposals quite different from the Democratic and Green parties.

Democratic Left: Bernie Sanders and Defeating the Oligarchy

The context for Bernie Sanders education proposals, as stated in his 2016 campaign book *Our Revolution: A Future to Believe In*, was the claim that the wealthy "want to move our country toward an oligarchic form of society in which all economic and political power rests with a handful of multibillionaire families."[2] Using income distribution charts, Sanders demonstrated increasing income inequality and the decline of the middle class. Sanders argued that the economic and political system was not working for the poor and middle class as wealth became more concentrated and Supreme Court rulings allowed more money to flow from the rich into campaign coffers. He asserted, "[I]t is not just a grotesque level of wealth disparity that we are experiencing. It is also horrendous inequality in terms of income, the amount we earn each year. Incredibly, in the last several years, 52 percent of all new income being generated in this country is now going to the top 1 percent."[3]

Higher education, against this background of growing disparities in wealth and political power, becomes, according to Sanders, a primary means of upper mobility for low-income and middle-class youth. However, a combination of increasing college costs and student loans has made higher education less affordable. As an example, Sanders claimed: "In 1978 it was possible to earn enough money to pay for a year of college tuition just by working a full-time summer job that paid minimum wage. Today, it would take a minimum-wage worker an entire year to earn enough to cover the average annual in-state tuition at a public university—if that worker had no other expenses at all for that year."[4]

The political pressure of the rising oligarchy, he argued, was responsible for a decline of higher education funding and resulting increases in tuition. Contributing to increasing tuition, Sanders argued, was the growing number of college administrators in contrast to the declining number of professors and increasing use of adjuncts. He reminded the reader that, back in the 1960s and 1970s, tuition at state and city universities was very low, and in the case of the City University of New York, there were no tuition fees. High tuition costs have forced students, Sanders asserted, to rely more and more on student loans. "Growing student debt," he argued, "is one of the major reasons young people are delaying getting married and having kids, and why families are putting off buying homes, starting businesses and saving for retirement. This, in turn, is slowing overall economic growth."[5]

To correct the problem, Sanders offered what he called the College for All Act to create a partnership between the federal government and states, where the federal government would give states $2 for every $1 states spent on colleges and universities. The goal was to make state higher education tuition free. "The plan," he wrote, "would also cover 100 percent of the cost books and room and board for low-income students."[6]

How would the federal government pay for the subsidy to make state higher education tuition free? He proposed a financial transaction tax on investment houses and hedge funds: "A financial transaction tax of just 0.5 percent on stock trades (that's 50 cents for every $100 worth of stock), a 0.1 percent fee on bonds, and a 0.005 percent on derivatives would raise up to $300 billion a year, significantly more revenue than my college plan would require."[7] The proposed College for All Act would allow students to refinance their student debt, as discussed in Chapter 4.

Bernie Sanders call for free tuition at state higher education institutions and concerns about student debt found their way into, as discussed in Chapter 4, the 2016 Democratic platform and Hillary Clinton's campaign. However, missing from both platform and Clinton campaign was Sander's proposal to pay for it by taxing Wall Street investment firms and hedge funds. Also, missing was his sharp criticism of the rise of oligarchy in the United States.

Green Party: Educating Critical and Active Citizens

In 2016, the Green Party emphasized education for sustainable economic development in contrast to the Republican's emphasis on free markets and the human capital education theories of Democrats. The 2016 Green Party platform argued that society should be considered part of nature and not separate from it. Their platform explains economic sustainability as: "We must maintain an ecological balance and live within the ecological and resource limits of our communities and our planet. We support a sustainable society that utilizes resources in such a way that future generations will benefit and not suffer from the practices of our generation."[8]

Sustainability and citizenship education was the major thrust of the 2016 Green Party education platform that called on the country, "to educate ourselves to build a just, sustainable, humane and democratic future, and to become responsible and effective citizens of the local and global communities."[9] Unlike the Democratic and Republican education proposals, the 2016 Green Party stressed citizenship education, including development of critical thinkers. It also stressed holistic education.

For the 2016 Green Party, the goal is education of active citizens something missing from the Democratic and Republican education agendas. The party platform framed it this way: "Greens believe every child deserves a public education that fosters critical and holistic thought, and provides the breadth and depth of learning necessary to become an *active citizen and a constructive member of our society* [author's emphasis]".[10]

The Green Party also rejected the idea that education, unlike Democrats, should focus on job preparation and growing the economy: "Greens believe in education, not indoctrination. We do not think that schools should turn our children into servile students, employees, consumers or citizens."[11] The emphasis on active citizenship is included in the 2016 platform's section on recommended actions: "Include a vigorous and engrossing civics curriculum in later elementary and secondary schools, to teach students to be active citizens."[12] The Green Party's inclusion of "servile . . . consumers" reflected a historic concern of the Green Party with consumer capitalism. Consumerism, as I discuss later in this chapter, is a historic concern of the Green Party.

The Green Party's concern with educating active citizens reflects a concept of grassroots democracy, which makes a distinction between representative government and direct democracy. The democratic aspect of representative government is the right of citizens to vote for their representatives. In contrast, the 2016 platform lists as a core value: "Participatory Democracy, rooted in community practice at the grassroots level and informing every level, from the local to the international."[13]

Since its founding, the Green Party has supported participatory democracy over representative government. The 1996 Green Party explained:

> Greens advocate direct democracy as a response to local needs and issues, where all concerned citizens can discuss and decide questions that immediately affect their lives, such as land use, parks, schools and community services. We hold as a "key value" GRASSROOTS DEMOCRACY and, as such, would decentralize many state functions to the country level and seek expanded roles for neighborhood boards/associations.[14]

The 2016 Green Party platform lists "Grassroots Democracy" as number one on their list of "10 Key Values." The 2016 platform states:

1. Grassroots Democracy

   All human beings must be allowed a say in decisions that affect their lives; no one should be subject to the will of another. We work to improve public participation in every aspect of government and seek to ensure that our public representatives are fully accountable to the people who elect them. *We also work to create new types of political organizations that expand the process of participatory democracy by directly including citizens in decision-making* [author's emphasis].[15]

In other words, the Green Party envisioned schools educating students for maximum participation in the control of their own lives and the governing institutions that affect their lives. Consequently, unlike the education agendas of the two major political parties, the Green Party advocated that schools: "Include a vigorous and engrossing civics curriculum in later elementary and secondary schools, to teach students to be active citizens."[16]

The Green Party platform was concerned with the increased privatization and corporatization of public schools resulting from No Child Left Behind and the Race to the Top. The 2016 platform specifically complained about the involvement of certain foundations in the privatization of public schools: "We also call attention to the results of a quarter century of corporate funding from the likes of the Bradley and Wal-Mart Family Foundations—a vast, well-endowed and lucrative sector which seeks to dismantle, privatize, or militarize public education and destroy teachers unions."[17]

The platform also warned about the privatization of public education: "Regimes of high-stakes standardized testing and the wholesale diversion of resources away from public schools are provoking crises for which the bipartisan corporate consensus recommends school closings, dissolution of entire school districts and replacement by unaccountable, profit-based charter schools. The Green Party is unalterably opposed to the dissolution of public schools and the privatization of education."[18] Consequently, a recommended action of the 2016 platform was: "Oppose the administration of public schools by private, for-profit entities."[19]

There is a warning in the platform about militarization of schools. This, in part, is a reference to No Child Left Behind, which opened school records to military recruiters. The 2004 Green Party platform was more specific: "The Leave No Child Behind Act must be repealed, especially the section that gives the military access to student records."[20] The 2016 platform provides a more expansive condemnation of what the Greens call the "militarization of schools":

> We demand an end to the militarization of our schools. J-ROTC programs are an expensive drain on our limited educational resources and a diversion from their important mission to prepare our young to assume their role in a peaceful tomorrow. ASVAB[21] testing is being used to mine public school student bodies for data to support military recruiting. Forbid military access to student records. The Pentagon's Recruitment Command is misdirecting public tax dollars on manipulative campaigns that prey on our young. We insist that local education authorities stand up to these destructive practices.[22]

The 2016 Green Party called for action regarding equality of educational opportunity: "Eliminate gross inequalities in school funding. Federal policy on education should act principally to provide equal access to a quality education."[23] The proposal for federal policy to ensure equality of educational opportunity was consistent with previous Green Party statements, such as that of the 2004 Green Party platform's assertion that: "Federal policy on education should act principally to ensure equal access to a quality education."[24]

A striking feature of the 2016 Green Party platform is its dropping of past support for choice within public schools. In the opening to the "Education" section of their 2004 platform, it was asserted that: "Greens support educational diversity. We hold no dogma absolute, continually striving for truth in the realm of ideas."[25] Reflecting a view that intellectual diversity is important for social progress, the 2004 platform asserted the importance of school choice: "Education starts with choice, and within public education we believe in broad choices. Magnet schools, Site-based Management, Schools within Schools, alternative models, and parental involvement are ways in which elementary education can be changed to make a real difference in the lives of our children."[26]

However, the 2004 platform did reject the use of vouchers for privately operated charter schools: "We oppose vouchers, or any scheme that will transfer money out of the public school system. . . . We also oppose charter schools or the administration of public schools by private, for-profit entities."[27] The 2004 platform asserted that vouchers and privately operated charter schools would result in "a separate and unequal educational system."[28] But, the Green Party has consistently supported home schooling as stated in their 2016 platform: "Recognize the viable alternative of home-based education."[29]

While not supporting vouchers or other choice plans as a method for providing diverse forms of education, the 2016 Green Party did support diverse programs in public schools. The 2016 platform called for promotion of: "diverse set of educational opportunities, including bi-lingual education, continuing education, job retraining, distance learning, mentoring and apprenticeship programs."[30]

Green Party: Art Education and Political Activism

A distinguishing feature of the Green Party was promotion of arts education to improve social, environmental and political conditions. No other political party emphasized the importance of the arts for improving the quality of society. The wording of the arts section of the Green Party platform has remained pretty much the same from 2004 to 2016. It is included in the same part of platform as education: "E. Education and the Arts." The opening lines of the art section of the 2016 platform expresses the belief that art is important for political empowerment and sustainability of the environment: "Freedom of artistic expression is a fundamental right and a key element in *empowering communities*, and in *moving us toward sustainability* and respect for diversity [author's emphasis]."[31]

There is an important political dimension to this advocacy of arts education. The closest encounter I've had with this linkage between politics and art education is in the writings of Maxine Greene.[32] The statement included in these Green platforms that links art to politics was:

> Artists can create in ways that foster healthy, non-alienating relationships between people and their daily environments, communities, and the Earth. This can include both artists whose themes advocate compassion, nurturance, or cooperation; and artists *whose creations unmask the often-obscure connections between various forms of violence, domination, and oppression, or effectively criticize aspects of the very community that supports their artistic activity* [author's emphasis].[33]

The Green Party included in the term "art" a wide variety of art education activities: "Diversity in arts education in the schools including age-specific hands-on activities and appreciative theoretical approaches, exposure to the arts of various cultures and stylistic traditions, and experiences with a variety of media, techniques and contents."[34]

It is through exposure and the practice of different art forms that students learn to see the world in different ways, including breaking through the dominant view of society to lay bare its inner workings and connections. In addition, art was to help students imagine better forms of political organization, which would contribute to civic education and social activism.

Thus, art education fits the overall goal of the Green Party's education agenda for a "public education that fosters critical and holistic thought."[35] Holistic thought refers to seeing the world as an interactive system with each part dependent on the other. Thus, protection of the environment was part of a holistic view of the interaction of humans with nature and with the forces of nature interacting with each other. According to the Green Party, arts education contributed to this holistic view: "The integration of the arts and artistic teaching methods into other areas of the curriculum to promote a holistic perspective."[36]

In order for the arts to influence political and environmental conditions, the Green Party asserted: "The arts can only perform their social function if they are completely free from outside control."[37] The Green Party platform called for increased local, state and federal funding of the arts "appropriate to their essential social role."[38] To ensure funding does not censor the social function of art, the platform stated: "Eliminating all laws that seek to restrict or censor artistic expression, including the withholding of government funds for political or moral content."[39]

Green Party: Sustainability and Consumerism

Protecting the environment is a central focus of the Green Party. As mentioned earlier in the chapter, the Green Party prefaced its education agenda with a call to educate for a sustainable future. The Green Party defined sustainability as achieving a balance between economic growth and protecting the environment. Greens criticized the attitude that nature or the biosphere was something for humans to conquer to serve their own interests rather than recognizing that humans are part of nature and dependent on its existence. The Green Party platform asserts that both communist and capitalist systems operate to advance economic growth without consideration of the impact on the environment.

> The human community is an element of the Earth community, not the other way around. All human endeavors are situated within the dynamics of the biosphere. If we wish to have sustainable institutions and enterprises, they must fit well with the processes of the Earth. The ideology of industrialism, in both capitalist and communist countries, insists that modern society lives on top of nature and should rightly use and despoil the rest of

the natural world as we desire—because any loss of the ecosystems is merely an "externality" in economic thought and because any problems can be addressed later by a technological fix. We are now living through the painful consequences of that arrogant, ignorant perspective. Many of our children suffer from accumulations of mercury and other toxins in their neurological systems, environmentally related cancer is on the rise, and our air and water are increasingly polluted. Meanwhile, our ecosystems are being compromised by the spreading presence of genetically engineered organisms.[40]

When the Green Party referred to capitalism, it primarily meant "consumer" capitalism. In the 2000 presidential election, long-time consumer advocate Ralph Nader was the Green Party candidate. Nader was the first U.S. presidential candidate to focus on the problems associated with a consumerist ideology. Nader's educational concern was with the impact of consumerist ideology on children and teenagers and what he considered the resulting undermining of democratic activism.

Consumerist ideology assumes that the goal of the economic system is constant growth and consumption of products. Within this framework, the goal of technological development is the production of new goods. However, the production of new goods requires the creation of new human needs. The development of advertising techniques in the United States in the early 20th century, and the global spread of these techniques in the 20th and 21st centuries, is the agency for developing these new needs. Economists, such as Simon Patten in the early 20th century, argued that agricultural and industrial development would continually produce surpluses of products. The only way the agricultural and industrial machinery could be maintained, Patten argued, was the creation of new needs.[41] Later, corporations, such as General Motors, introduced the idea of planned obsolescence through advertising new styles and models.

Consequently, advertising not only created a need for new products but also convinced consumers to abandon products that they own for similar products with different styling. Within the framework of consumerism ideology, personal identity and social status are attached to brand names. People proudly wear clothes with identifying brand names or drive cars that identify their personality or social status.

Working and spending are the central values of consumerist ideology. Constant consumption requires longer hours of work. This is the tragic irony of consumerism. Technological advances do not free people from work but instead make new products that require more work to purchase. For instance, technology could be used to produce durable goods and reduce hours at work.

Commodified leisure, as exemplified by movies, television, Disney World, video games, recreational products and packaged travel, provide both an escape from work and a reason to work harder. People work harder so that they can buy such items as boats, golf clubs, the newest hiking gear and tickets for travel on a cruise ship. The desire for commodified leisure fills the fantasy world of the worker. In turn, the consumption of leisure provides escape from the often-numbing quality of office and factory work.

What distinguishes consumer capitalism? Often, capitalism assumes that people make rational choices in a free market. But consumer capitalism sees advertising manipulating individual choices in the market. In turn, political choices are the result of the manipulation of desires through the media. Politicians rely on advertising, media experts and spin doctors to present their political agenda. Political image takes the place of political substance.

Green Party: Ralph Nader, Consumerism and Education

During the 2000 presidential campaign, Nader made consumerism a central piece of his educational policy statements. In his presidential acceptance speech on June 25, 2000, Nader argued that there is a responsibility "to ensure that our children are well cared for. This is an enormous undertaking because our children are now exposed to the most intense marketing onslaught in history."[42] This marketing offensive, Nader argued, involves "precise corporate selling . . . beamed directly to children separating them from their parents, an unheard of practice formerly, and teaching them how to nag their beleaguered parents as unpaid salesman for companies. There is a bombardment of their impressionable minds."[43]

Nader linked the lack of political activism and concern among youth to the commercialization of their minds. He argued that commodified leisure occupies more and more of children's time. This results, Nader contended, in youth not responding to the growing economic inequalities in the United States and between nations. "To the youth of America," Nader warned in his acceptance speech, "beware of being trivialized by the commercial culture that tempts you daily. I hear you saying often that you're not turned on to politics. . . . If you do not turn on to politics, politics will turn on you."[44]

For Nader, commodified leisure reduced political activity and interfered with the ability of children to learn. Nader argued, "Obviously, you see how our children are not learning enough history, they're not learning how to write. Their attention span is being shrunken by all this entertainment on TV and videos that are beamed to them."[45] In his nomination speech, he contended that, "This does not prepare the next generation to become literate, self-renewing, effective citizens for a deliberative democracy."[46]

The problem, as Nader defined it, was corporate targeting of children as present and future consumers. He quoted Mike Searles, former president of Kids-R-Us: "If you own this child at an early age, you can own this child for years to come. Companies are saying, 'Hey, I want to own the kid younger and younger.'"[47] To prove his point, he quoted a *Los Angeles Times* interview with Nancy Shalek, president of the Shalek Agency: "Advertising at its best is making people feel that without their product, you're a loser. Kids are very sensitive to that. . . . You open up emotional vulnerabilities and it's very easy to do with kids because they're the most emotionally vulnerable."[48]

The undermining of parental authority, according to Nader, was the goal of advertisers and their paid child psychologists. Boys and girls under the age of 12, Nader claimed, were responsible for the spending of $25 billion a year. Nader contended that marketers use three methods to "avoid or neutralize parental authority":

> First, they urge the child to nag the parents.
>
> Second, the sellers take conscious advantage of the absence of parents who are commuting and working long hours away from home.
>
> Third, the marketers know that if they can undermine the authority, dignity, and judgment of parents in the eyes of their children, the little ones will purchase or demand items regardless of their parents' opinions.[49]

In addition to being disturbed by the undermining of democracy by training of present and future consumers, Nader was disturbed by the effects of advertising and media on the present and future health of children. For instance, he argued that there was a direct link between teenage drinking and car crashes, suicide, date rapes and problems teenagers have had in school and with their parents. Despite these problems, the alcohol industry advertises to audiences, according to the Federal Trade Commission, that include children and places their products in PG and PG-13 films that appeal to children and teenagers. In addition, the alcohol industry advertised on eight of the fifteen television shows that were most popular with adolescents.[50]

Violence is, Nader contended, presented to children and teenagers through movies, television and video games. Nader quoted Lt. Col. Grossman, coauthor of *Stop Teaching Our Kids to Kill*, that shooter video games such as Duke Nukem, Time Crisis and Quake "teach children the motor skills to kill, like military training devices do. And then they turn around and teach them to like it like the military would never do."[51]

Also, according Nader, children's health was undermined by a "barrage of ads for Whoppers, Happy Meals, Coke, Pepsi, Snickers bars, M&M's, and other junk foods and fast foods."[52] These marketing efforts contribute to the rise of child and teenage obesity and diabetes. Heath risks associated with severe obesity among children, Nader claimed, has doubled since the 1960s.

What was Nader's answer to the destruction of democracy through the commercialization of the minds of children and teenagers? First, he argued that Congress should repeal Public Law 96-252, which prohibits the Federal Trade Commission from establishing rules to the protect children from commercial advertising. Second, he appealed for a coalition of groups, including conservative organizations such as the Eagle Forum and Family Research Council, to work for laws to protect children from advertising and limit the access of marketing groups to public schools. Third, he urged citizens to join the Center for a New American Dream, which was dedicated to overthrowing the ideology of consumerism. He recommended that citizens obtain the Center for a New American Dream's pamphlet, "Tips for Parenting in a Commercial Culture."

The Nader campaign also stressed the issue of child poverty, contending that 20 percent of children in the U.S. lived in poverty—a figure much higher than that for any other Western country. In addition, there is a direct link, Nader contended, between childhood poverty and school performance and, consequently, expectations for future earnings. Childhood poverty contributes, Nader argued, to the perpetuation of poverty. Nader called for more expanded health and welfare programs for children that would be paid for out of the future budget surplus of the federal government.

Nader was the first presidential candidate to directly attack the ideology of consumerism and propose an educational agenda that included the protection of children and teenagers from indoctrination into consumerist values. This protection was to be combined with the teaching of an anti-consumerist ideology that included environmental education. In addition, Nader urged government programs to eliminate childhood poverty. The combination of these efforts, Nader believed, would result in a generation dedicated to hands-on participation in democratic processes.

Concern about sustainability and consumerism continued as a theme of the Green Party. In the context of education, one goal was to protect students from advertising similar to the issues raised by Ralph Nader. For instance, the 2004 Green Party platform stated: "We are deeply concerned about the intervention in our schools of corporations that promote a culture of consumption and waste. Schools should not be vehicles for commercial advertising."[53] In 2010, the Green Party platform provided a more abbreviated version: "Prohibit advertising to children in schools. Corporations should not be allowed to use the schools as vehicles for commercial advertising or corporate propaganda."[54]

A broader statement appeared in the 2016 platform: "Prohibit commercial advertising targeted to children less than 12 years old, as well as advertising in public places such as schools, parks, and government buildings."[55] The platform also called for a removal of advertising in educational institutions: "Young people should be kept free from coercive advertising at their educational institutions."[56] In the educational section of the 2016 platform, the Green Party called for prohibiting "advertising to children in schools. Corporations should not be allowed to use the schools as vehicles for commercial advertising or corporate propaganda."[57]

In summary, the Green Party's education agenda is in sharp contrast with the Republican and Democratic Parties. Neither Democrats or Republicans included in their agendas educating active citizens to bring about social change and to work for sustainability. In contrast to educating for a holistic view of environmental and social problems and for ways of imagining a better future, the Republican Party retains its traditional concerns with patriotic and character education, including abstinence sex education, and the Democratic Party trumpets education as the solution for poverty and income inequality.

The Libertarian Party: Separation of School and State

The Libertarian Party offers an alternative vision that is very close to that championed by Republican Secretary of Education Betsy DeVos as discussed in Chapter 1. The Libertarian Party was dedicated, as stated in their 2016 platform, to "a world of liberty; a world in which all individuals are sovereign over their own lives and no one is forced to sacrifice his or her values for the benefit of others."[58] In language that Secretary of Education Betsy DeVos might agree to, the 2016 platform championed a highly individualistic society: "We hold that all individuals have the right to exercise sole dominion over their own lives, and have the right to live in whatever manner they choose, so long as they do not forcibly interfere with the equal right of others to live in whatever manner they choose."[59]

Sounding very much like DeVos, without the Christian agenda, the education section of the 2016 Libertarian platform declares:

> Education is best provided by the free market, achieving greater quality, accountability and efficiency with more diversity of choice. Recognizing that the education of children is a parental responsibility, we would restore authority to parents to determine the education of their children, without interference from government. *Parents should have control of and responsibility for all funds expended for their children's education* [author's emphasis].[60]

The parallels between DeVos and Libertarians is not surprising given, as I discuss in Chapter 1, that both Betsy DeVos and her husband Richard are committed to a free market economy.

In Chapter 1, I discussed the influence of Friedrich Hayek's free market theories on the Republican's support of educational choice, including vouchers for use at both public and private schools. However, in general, the Republican Party, Betsy DeVos maybe the exception, has not supported a complete free market for education that turns schools over to market choices with all schools operating for-profit and dependent for their existence on parental choice. This type of free educational market would allow for any type of curriculum, subject and teaching method to exist as long as it was supported by parental choice. In other words, if no parent wanted a particular curriculum, subject or teaching method then it would not survive.

Theoretically, an educational free market would remove political control of the curriculum. This would mean abolishment of government curricula like the Common Core State Standards and the attempt by state and federal governments to have schools serve the interests of the economy. A free market for education would contribute to a free market of ideas with, at least theoretically, the best ideas surviving. The progress of society would thus be a function of the best ideas that survive the competition of the marketplace.

Concern about the use of schools to push a political agenda appeared in the Western world in the 19th century as public schooling became popular. Max Stirner (1806–1856) warned that controlling dissemination of ideas through schools was fast becoming central to the governing processes of modern nation-states. Stirner's phrase "wheels in the head" refers to ideas that schools (and now media and information technology) consciously intend to implant in human minds as a means of controlling behavior. These wheels in the head own the individual rather than the individual owning the idea. In his classic volume *The Ego and His Own: The Case of the Individual Against Authority* (1845), Stirner wrote about wheels in the head: "The thought is my own only when I have no misgiving about bringing it in danger of death every moment, when I do not have to fear its loss as a loss for me, a loss of me."[61] In other words, public schools were a new instrument of government domination designed to control the thinking and actions of citizens.

In the late 19th century, John Stuart Mill gave voice to a similar idea when he argued that government-operated schools are designed to serve the interests of power by controlling the minds and bodies of citizens. He wrote,

> A general State education is a mere contrivance for molding people to be exactly like one another: and as the mold in which it casts them is that which pleases the predominant power in the government, whether this be a monarch, a priesthood, an aristocracy, or the majority of the existing genera-tion, in proportion as it is efficient and successful, *it establishes a despotism over the mind, leading by natural tendency to one over the body* [author's emphasis].[62]

Reflecting the concern about political control of citizen's minds through pub-lic schooling, the Libertarian Party's 2000 platform called for separation of school and state: "We advocate the complete separation of education and State. Govern-ment schools lead to the indoctrination of children and interfere with the free choice of individuals."[63] The platform called for ending all government involve-ment in education: "Government ownership, operation, regulation, and subsidy of schools and colleges should be ended. We call for the repeal of the guarantees of tax-funded, government-provided education, which are found in most state constitutions."[64]

Appeals for separation of school and state continued to be a major theme of among Libertarians. For instance, writing on the Libertarian Solutions website, Austin Raynor asserted: "The Need to Abolish Public Education." He wrote,

> Contrary to general sentiment, we are doing a disservice to our children by continuing to support public education. Markets consistently produce

better and more consumer-oriented results than do monopolies or bureaucracies, a rule which applies to schooling just as it does to any other sector. But it is a built-in defense mechanism of the flawed schooling system that it is able to indoctrinate citizens to not question its existence; public schooling itself is the largest propaganda campaign in history. It is a government's dream. But on both a moral and pragmatic basis it must be rejected.[65]

Of course, separation of school and state would mean abolishing compulsory education laws as called for in by the Libertarian Party in 2000: "We advocate the complete separation of education and State. Government schools lead to the indoctrination of children and interfere with the free choice of individuals. Government ownership, operation, regulation, and subsidy of schools and colleges should be ended. We call for the repeal of the guarantees of tax-funded, government-provided education, which are found in most state constitutions."[66]

Separation of school and state included ending compulsory education laws as stated in its 2000 platform: "We condemn compulsory education laws, which spawn prison-like schools with many of the problems associated with prisons, and we call for an immediate repeal of such laws. Until government involvement in education is ended, we support elimination, within the governmental school system, of forced busing and corporal punishment. We further support immediate reduction of tax support for schools, and removal of the burden of school taxes from those not responsible for the education of children."[67]

In its 2008 platform, the Libertarian Party declared: "Education is best provided by the free market, achieving greater quality and efficiency with more diversity of choice. Schools should be managed locally to achieve greater accountability and parental involvement. Recognizing that the education of children is inextricably linked to moral values, we would return authority to parents to determine the education of their children, without interference from government. Parents should have control of all funds expended for their children's education."[68]

While calling for the separation of school and state, the Libertarian Party asserted that: "Poor children suffer the most under the current education system. Wealthy parents can afford to send their children to better or safer schools. Poor parents have no choice. Their children generally end up in the schools with the worst problems. These children end up at a public school, which is obligated to accept every local student, even those who are not interested in learning or who have a reputation for being disruptive or dangerous. The current system traps poor children in poor schools."[69]

Its 2015 platform directly criticized President Barack Obama's Race to the Top's efforts to create world-class schools: "Mr. President, we can have world-class education. The first step is defunding and eliminating the federal Department of Education, abolishing Common Core, and allowing parents to take full control over their children's education. Free-market competition will raise educational standards, lower costs, and prepare students to compete in a global economy."[70]

Conclusion: Oligarchy, Saving the Planet and the Education Marketplace

In the 2016 election, Bernie Sanders, unlike other candidates, was willing to link education policies to the increasing concentration of wealth, income inequalities and the political power of the oligarchy. His criticism was highlighted in 2017, when President Donald Trump selected a cabinet composed mainly of billionaires and multimillionaires, including billionaire Betsy DeVos as Secretary of Education.[71] Was Bernie Sanders correct that education policies would now favor the interests of the oligarchy?

One alternative to oligarchic power was the Green Party. The Green Party favored maximizing political participation and grassroots democracy by educating students for civic activism. The goal of public school education for civic activism was absent from the Democratic, Republican and Libertarian education agendas.

The Green and Libertarian parties are concerned about education being used as an instrument of ideological domination. The Green Party fears that current federal education policies will result in creating servile workers for corporations and passive citizens. The Green Party wants to overcome the use of schools for ideological control by maximizing local control; emphasizing education for civic activism; and expanding art education to unveil social, economic and political oppression and open student imaginations to find new ways of achieving social progress. Libertarians would like to break the bonds of ideological domination by political forces by separating school and state and turn education over to the forces of the marketplace.

The Green Party advocates education for sustainable development and criticizes the growth of consumer capitalism with its throwaway culture and endless quest to produce more products for consumption. Greens particularly criticize advertising targeted at children and advertising in schools.

In contrast, the Libertarians put concerns about the environment in the framework of the free market and limiting government power. Given their desire to separate school and state, there are no calls for environmental education. However, from a Libertarian standpoint, environmental education might be something chosen by parents in a free market of schools. The 2012 Libertarian platform states: "We support a clean and healthy environment and sensible use of our natural resources. . . . *Free markets and property rights stimulate the technological innovations and behavioral changes required to protect our environment and ecosystems* [author's emphasis]."[72]

The Green Party provides an important alternative to the education agendas of the Democratic and Republican Parties. On the other hand, it might be difficult to separate the thinking of Libertarian Party leaders from that of Republican Secretary of Education Betsy DeVos. The major difference might be the secular emphasis of the Libertarian Party in contrast to the Christian ideology of Betsy DeVos. However, at this point in time, it appears that federal education policy will be dominated by the oligarchy warned about by Bernie Sanders.

Notes

1 Alex Seitz-Wald, "Clinton Adopts Key Piece of Sanders Student Debt Plan. "*NBC News*, July 6, 2016. Retrieved from www.nbcnews.com/politics/2016-election/clin ton-adopts-key-piece-sanders-student-debt-plan-n604621 on January 30, 2017.
2 Bernie Sanders, *Our Revolution: A Future to Believe In* (New York: Saint Martin's Press, 2016), p. 188.
3 Ibid., p. 208.
4 Ibid., pp. 344–345.
5 Ibid., p. 346.
6 Ibid., p. 348.
7 Ibid., pp. 349–350.
8 "Platform 2016 Green Party of the United States," p. 5. Retrieved from https://d3n8a8p ro7vhmx.cloudfront.net/gpus/pages/4899/attachments/original/1479737472/2016-Green-Party-platform.pdf?1479737472 on January 26, 2017.
9 Ibid., p. 28.
10 Ibid.
11 Ibid.
12 Ibid., p. 29.
13 Ibid., p. 4.
14 The 1996 Green platform, "IV. platform Policy Document: Democracy: B. Political Participation." Retrieved from www.greenparty.org on February 1, 2001.
15 "Platform 2016 Green Party of the United States. . . ., " p. 5.
16 Ibid., p. 28.
17 Ibid.
18 Ibid.
19 Ibid.
20 Green Party of the United States, "2004 platform as Adopted at the National Nominating Convention, Milwaukee, Wisconsin," June, 2004, p. 28. Retrieved from www. gp.org/platform/2004/2004platform.pdf on May 16, 2013.
21 The ASVAB is a multiple-aptitude battery that measures developed abilities and helps predict future academic and occupational success in the military. It is administered annually to more than one million military applicants, high school and post-secondary students. Retrieved from the Official Site of the ASVAB, http://official-asvab.com/ on May 16, 2013.
22 Ibid., p. 29.
23 Ibid., p. 28.
24 "Green Party of the United States, 2004 platform. . . ," p. 28.
25 Ibid., p. 27.
26 Ibid.
27 Ibid., p. 28.
28 Ibid.
29 "Platform 2016 Green Party of the United States. . . ," p. 29.
30 Ibid., p. 28.

31 Ibid., p. 29.
32 See Maxine Green, *Releasing the Imagination: Essays on Education, the Arts, and Social Change* (New York: Jossey-Bass, 2000).
33 "Platform 2016 Green Party of the United States...," p. 29.
34 Ibid.
35 Ibid., p. 28.
36 Ibid., p. 29.
37 Ibid.
38 Ibid.
39 Ibid.
40 Ibid., p. 40.
41 Simon N. Patten, *The New Basis of Civilization* (Cambridge, MA: Harvard University Press, 1968).
42 Ralph Nader, "Children and Education." Retrieved from http://votenader.org. on January 22, 2001.
43 Ibid.
44 Ibid.
45 Ibid.
46 Ibid.
47 Ralph Nader, "Why Is the Government Protecting Corporations That Prey on Kids?" Retrieved from http://votenader.org on September 22, 1999.
48 Ibid.
49 Ralph Nader, "Making Parents Irrelevant." Retrieved from http:// votenader.org on October 27, 1999.
50 Nader, "Why Is the Government...."
51 Ibid.
52 Ibid.
53 "Green Party of the United States, 2004 platform...," p. 27.
54 "Green Party of the United States platform 2010 as Adopted by the Green National Committee," p. 27. Retrieved from www.gp.org/committees/platform/2010/index.php on May 14, 2013.
55 "Platform 2016 Green Party of the United States...," p. 11.
56 Ibid., p. 24.
57 Ibid., p. 28.
58 "Libertarian Party platform as Adopted in Convention," May 2016, Orlando, Florida, p. 1. Retrieved from www.lp.org/platform/ on October 21, 2016.
59 Ibid., p. 1.
60 Ibid., p. 5.
61 Max Stirner, *The Ego and His Own: The Case of the Individual Against Authority*, trans. Steven T. Byington (New York: Libertarian Book Club, 1963), p. 342.
62 John Stuart Mill, *On Liberty* (Indianapolis, IN: The Liberal Arts Press, 1956), p. 129.
63 On the Issues, "Libertarian Party on Education." Retrieved from www.ontheissues.org/celeb/Libertarian_Party_Education.htm on May 14, 2013.
64 Ibid.
65 Austin Raynor, "The Need to Abolish Public Education," The Libertarian Solution. Retrieved from www.libertariansolution.com/liberty-library/012/the-need-to-abolish-public-education on May 16, 2013.
66 On the Issues, "The Libertarian Party's Legislative Program," November 7, 2000. Retrieved from www.ontheissues.org/celeb/Libertarian_Party_Education.htm on January 30, 2017.
67 Ibid.
68 Ibid.

69 Ibid.

70 Ibid.

71 Julianna Goldman, "Donald Trump's Cabinet Richest in U.S. History, Historians Say," *CBS NEWS*, December 20, 2016. Retrieved from www.cbsnews.com/news/donald-trump-cabinet-richest-in-us-history-historians-say/ on February 1, 2017.

72 "Libertarian Party platform as Adopted in Convention. . . ," p. 4.

6

NEW AGENDA FOR AMERICAN SCHOOLS

I am proposing a New Agenda for American schools that brings together proposals I have made in other contexts. These proposals include an amendment to the U.S. Constitution, replacing the current human capital paradigm dominating educational policy, and a renewed emphasis on holistic environmental education. My New Agenda for American Schools answers important issues raised by Republican, Democratic, Green and Libertarian parties.

Issues Requiring a New Agenda for American Schools

None of the federal education legislation since the 2001 No Child Left Behind resulted in any significant improvement in U.S. schools. No Child Left Behind created an era of teaching to the test, test prep and boycotts led by the parent-driven Opt Out movement to keep their kids home on testing day. During Democratic President Barack Obama's tenure, doors were thrown open to investment and for-profit education companies. The creation of a national curriculum, Common Core State Standards, was rejected by some states and by the 2016 Republican campaign. It wasn't even mentioned in the 2016 Democratic platform.

What remains after a decade of supposed school reform legislation, as discussed in previous chapters, is increased economic and racial segregation and expansion of charter schools, many with questionable success in educating students. As witnessed by the 2016 Republican platform, religious issues continue to be a force in shaping education policies. U.S. Secretary of Education Betsy DeVos exemplifies the continuing struggle, since the 1960s' school prayer and Bible decisions, to restore some aspect of Christian dogma in the schools.

I would argue that public education has not benefitted from these educational struggles, and as Bernie Sanders warned, education policies at the federal and state levels are increasingly controlled by an oligarchy of the rich who preach free market doctrines supporting school choice, vouchers and for-profit schools. While the Green Party might support civic education and teaching political activism, the 2016 Democratic and Republican parties never even suggest that civic education is important. Would an oligarchy want schools to educate students who might actively work to decrease the political power of wealth and increase grassroots democracy? I doubt it.

Based on human capital theory, Democrats keep recycling arguments that schools will reduce poverty, income inequality and grow the economy. As I've suggested there is no proof that investment in schools will do any of these things. In fact, I would argue, that Democrats, except for Bernie Sanders, cling to human capital theory to avoid other measures that might redistribute income to benefit the poor and create greater economic equality.

Therefore, I argue, public schools should be protected from political and economic forces wanting schools to serve their interests. To accomplish this, I propose an amendment to the U.S. Constitution to ensure equality of educational spending, limiting the political and religious imposition of ideas and protecting languages and cultures. Also, we should replace free market and human capital goals with one that stresses schooling as a way of maximizing people's ability to lead long and satisfying lives. And finally, we need a holistic environmental education, which, I would argue, helps humanity have long and satisfying lives.

New Agenda for American Schools: Constitutional Amendment

The U.S. Constitution was written before schooling became an important part of the social fabric. There is nothing in the U.S. Constitution about education and, consequently, the power over schooling has been given to state governments. One result is the inability of the federal government to mandate equal educational funding of public schools. This is highlighted by the ruling on school finance in the U.S. Supreme Court decision in *Rodriguez v. San Antonio School District* (1973). In this case, the U.S. Supreme Court refused to consider the issue of school finance, declaring, "The consideration and initiation of fundamental reforms with respect to state taxation and education are matters reserved for the legislative processes of the various states."[1]

Besides equal financing of education, it is important to protect the academic freedom of teachers to manage their own classrooms without outside interference from political and religious forces. Also, in response to the Republican agenda of "English-Only" and the long history of educational attempts to destroy the languages and cultures of conquered peoples, including Native Americans, Puerto Ricans, Hawaiians and Mexicans (northern part of Mexico conquered during the Mexican-American war), I would provide constitutional protection for languages and cultures.

I do not intend that my proposed amendment be fixed in stone. Like any other document it should be debated and changed.

Proposed Education Amendment to the U.S. Constitution

1. Everyone has the right to receive an education.
2. Primary, secondary and higher education shall be free.
3. Public schools will be equally financed.
4. Primary and secondary education shall be compulsory until the age of 16. The government will ensure through financial assistance, scholarships or other means that no one is denied an education or access to an educational institution because of lack of financial resources including resources for food, shelter and medical care.
5. Teachers in all government-operated schools will have the academic freedom to choose the methods of instruction and class materials to implement local curriculum requirements.
6. Local communities will have primary control over public school curricula and methods of instruction.
7. Everyone has a right to an education using the medium of their mother-tongue within a government-financed school system when the number of students requesting instruction in that mother-tongue equals the average number of students in a classroom in that government-financed school system.
8. Everyone has the right to learn the dominant or official language of the nation. The government-financed school system will make every effort to ensure that all students are literate in the dominant or official language of the country.

New Agenda for American Schools: Long Life and Happiness

In *A New Paradigm for Global School Systems: Education for Long Life and Happiness*,[2] I proposed a new global educational paradigm as an alternative to the increasingly criticized emphasis on education for economic growth and meeting labor market needs. In this paradigm, educational policy is focused on longevity and subjective well-being (happiness) rather than economic growth and personal income. These two objectives, while taking on different meanings in different cultures and religions, can be measured; they can be given concrete and objective meaning to guide public policy.

In my proposed goals for schooling, I am focusing on the social conditions that improve chances of living a long and satisfying life. There is ongoing community health and happiness research that will help achieve these goals. Currently global educational policy is centered on economic growth and preparing workers for the world's labor market. Economic growth is considered the measure of social progress. But these policies are increasingly criticized because of their negative effects on the quality of life. For instance, Nobel economist Amartya Sen is concerned with development policies focused solely on economic growth. In *Development as Freedom*, he uses longevity rates as a guide to the quality of human life.[3] Sen stresses that, "Since life expectancy variations relate to a variety of social opportunities that are central to development (including epidemiological policies, health care, educational facilities and so on), an income-centered view is in serious need of supplementation, in order to have a fuller understanding of the process of development."[4]

International studies of happiness or living a satisfying life find that money is important for the food, shelter and health care. On the other hand, extreme inequalities in wealth and the stress of competition contribute to a shorter life spans and unhappiness.[5] In the context of my proposed educational paradigm, income and jobs remain important for their contribution to longevity and happiness; people need food, shelter and health care.

Public health studies show that social inequality causes stress for those at bottom of a hierarchy, which in turn contributes to poor health, a reduced life span and a low sense of subjective well-being.[6] Stress in humans produces identifiable physical reactions resulting, among other things, in high blood pressure, heart disease and diabetes. As stress occurs, there is a rise in catecholamine, which causes an increase in blood pressure, pulse rate and a diversion of blood from the intestines. Also, stress increases levels of glucocorticoid, which increases blood sugar causing a resistance to insulin resulting in the possibility of adult-onset diabetes. There is also a change in fats in the blood causing low levels of HDL (the good cholesterol), increased plasma triglyceride, blood glucose and high blood pressure resulting in potential heart disease. Simply stated, stress reduces longevity.[7]

How does social inequality cause stress? The answer to this question takes us back to the notion of capabilities or as stated by Sen, "people's ability to lead the kind of lives they value—and have reason to value."[8] If you are at the bottom of most social hierarchies, you have less chance of leading the type of life you value, and consequently, you suffer the physical results of stress. And also, given the structure of most hierarchies such as corporations and government civil services, the "bicycling reaction" occurs, producing more stress.

Bicycling is an important image for understanding the effect of social hierarchies. The bicycle image is that of a person bending forward with hands on the handlebars while kicking back on the pedals. Or, in other words, bowing to authority while abusing those below. There is anger and stress caused by bowing to authority, and there is anger and stress caused in subordinates being kicked. Public health authority Richard Wilkinson quotes Volker Sommer, a distinguished primatologist, about how bicycling takes place in the animal world of which humans are a part: "It is very common in nonhuman primates that they, after having received aggression from a higher-ranking individual, will redirect aggression towards lower ranking ones. It can be a real chain reaction: Alpha slaps beta, beta slaps gamma, gamma slaps delta, delta slaps."[9] Wilkinson summarizes the bicycle reaction among humans: "There is a widespread tendency for those who have been most humiliated, who have had their sense of selfhood most reduced by low social status, to try to regain it by asserting their superiority over any weaker or more vulnerable groups."[10]

In *A New Paradigm for Global School Systems: Education for Long Life and Happiness*, I present a possible curriculum and textbook for providing the conditions for teachers and students to have a school experience that enhances their changes of having a long life and having satisfying school and lifetime experiences. I also suggest that the same principles be applied to the work of school teachers. Research suggests that anger about one's job and a lack of control over one's work contributes to a reduced life span. In other words, angry teachers do not benefit either teachers or students. Therefore, teachers' working conditions and control over their teaching material are important for creating satisfying learning experiences for students. In *A New Paradigm for Global School Systems*, I proposed the following:

Guidelines for a Global Core Curriculum

1. The curriculum should contain the knowledge and skills to maximize physical and mental health for living a long and happy life.
2. The curriculum should contain the knowledge and skills needed to maximize a person's capabilities to choose a life they value.
3. The curriculum should contain the knowledge and skills, including knowledge about research on the causal factors influencing longevity and subjective well-being, so that school graduates will be able to actively ensure that environmental, social, political and economic conditions promote a long and happy life for themselves and all other people.
4. The curriculum should contain knowledge and skills that will create the emotional desire and ethical belief in school graduates that will cause them to actively help others live a long and happy life.[11]

Guidelines for Global Methods of Instruction

1. Instructional methods should avoid increasing social inequalities between students.
2. Methods of instruction should enhance cooperation and trust between students and between students and teachers.
3. Methods of instruction should enhance optimal learning experiences or the joy of learning.[12]

Guidelines for Global School Organization

1. Schools should be organized to reduce the stress caused by the "bicycle syndrome." As part of reducing the effect of the bicycle syndrome, there should be a reduction—elimination would not be possible or necessarily desirable—of social inequalities between administrators, teachers and students.
2. Principles of trust and cooperation should permeate the school environment.
3. The environmental conditions of the school, including its architectural design, landscaping and availability of clean air, safe water and healthy food, should maximize the opportunity for administrators, teachers and students to live long and happy lives.
4. Whenever possible schools should include physical and mental health facilities that will maximize the health and subjective well-being of administrators, teachers and students.[13]

New Agenda for American Schools: Environmental Education

Environmental education contributes to long life and happiness by reducing the impact of pollution on people's health and the possibility of increased deaths and injuries from weather conditions caused by global climate change. In addition, the natural settings contribute to human happiness as evidenced by the creation and use of parks and pristine natural sites and the desire by people to hike, swim and stroll through natural settings.

I agree with the Green Party that there should be a holistic approach to environmental education that demonstrates the interrelationship of humans with nature and the impact of economic development on the biosphere. The concept of the biosphere, a key element of environmental education was introduced by Vladimir Vernadsky's 1926 book *The Biosphere* in which he criticized Western science for trying to understand nature by breaking it down into smaller and smaller parts.[14] Vernadsky caused a revolution in Western science by declaring, "Basically man cannot be separated from it [biosphere]; it is only now that this indissolubility begins to appear clearly and in precise terms before us. . . . Actually no living organism exists on earth in a state of freedom."[15] Vernadsky asserted, "All organisms are connected indissolubly and uninterruptedly, first of all through nutrition and respiration, with the circumambient material and energetic medium."[16]

Therefore, in *A New Paradigm for Global School Systems: Education for Long Life and Happiness*, I propose a global core curriculum that embodies environmental education.

Global Core Curriculum

1. The overarching framework for learning would be a human-centered biosphere.
2. The focus of learning should be on how the biosphere can promote human happiness and longevity.

3. The traditional subjects of the human capital curriculum along with environmental and human rights education would be integrated in holistic lessons that would:

   a. teach students the political, social and economic conditions that have decreased and increased human life spans and subjective well-being;
   b. require the use of problem-solving methods, including the use of imagination, to create conditions that promote a long life and happiness;
   c. give students the tools to change the world; and
   d. develop the ethical responsibility needed to protect happiness and lives of others.[17]

Conclusion: The Promise of a New Agenda for American Schools

My proposed constitutional amendment and education agenda is tentative, and I hope it will be refined through criticisms and discussions. We do need new thinking about the purposes of public education. There is little evidence that human capital education goals will result in economic growth, reduce income inequalities or even make the U.S. stronger in the world economy. The current emphasis on education for work or college neglects preparing students for participation in political institutions or civic activism. Current policies are increasing economic and racial segregation of students while turning school functions over to for-profit corporations.

Hopefully, my proposed constitutional amendment, new paradigm and holistic environmental education will spark a public debate that will lead to schools serving the interests of the people rather than the economic concerns of corporations.

Notes

1 Joel Spring, *American Education: An Introduction to Social and Political Aspects* (White Plains, NY: Longman, 1978), p. 228.
2 Joel Spring, *A New Paradigm for Global School Systems: Education for Long Life and Happiness* (Mahwah, NJ: Lawrence Erlbaum Associates, Publishers, 2007).
3 Amartya Sen, *Development as Freedom* (New York: Anchor Books, 2000).
4 Ibid., pp. 46–47.
5 See Spring, *A New Paradigm . . .*, pp. 37–71.
6 See Ichiro Kawachi and Bruce P. Kennedy, *The Health of Nations: Inequality Is Harmful to Your Health* (New York: The New Press, 2002); Michael Marmot, *The Status Syndrome: How Social Standing Affects Our Health and Longevity* (New York: Henry Holt and Company, 2004); and Richard Wilkinson, *The Impact of Inequality: How to Make Sick Societies Healthier* (New York: The New Press, 2005).
7 Marmot, *The Status Syndrome*, pp. 113–115.
8 Sen, *Development as Freedom*, p. 18.
9 See Wilkinson, *The Impact of Inequality*, p. 224.
10 Ibid., p. 225.
11 Spring, *A New Paradigm . . .*, p. 65.
12 Ibid., p. 66.

13 Ibid.
14 Lynton Keith Caldwell, *International Environmental Policy From the Twentieth to the Twenty-First Century: Third Edition* (Durham, NC: Duke University Press, 1996), pp. 24–25.
15 As quoted in Ibid., p. 26.
16 Ibid.
17 Spring, *A New Paradigm* . . ., p. 99.

INDEX